The Promise and Failure of Progressive Education

Norman Dale Norris

ScarecrowEducation
Lanham, Maryland • Toronto • Oxford
2004

Published in the United States of America
by ScarecrowEducation
An imprint of The Rowman & Littlefield Publishing Group, Inc.
4501 Forbes Boulevard, Suite 200, Lanham, Maryland 20706
www.scarecroweducation.com

PO Box 317
Oxford
OX2 9RU, UK

British Library Cataloguing in Publication Information Available

Library of Congress Cataloging-in-Publication Data

Norris, Norman Dale, 1958–
    The promise and failure of progressive education / Norman Dale Norris.
        p. cm.
    Includes bibliographical references ( ) and index.
    1-57886-115-2 (pbk. : alk. paper)
Progressive education — United States — History. 2. Education — United
States — Philosophy. 3. Student-centered learning — United States. I. Title.
    LB14.7 .N67 2004
    370'.1 22

                                                                2004007446

♾️™ The paper used in this publication meets the minimum requirements of
American National Standard for Information Sciences — Permanence of
Paper for Printed Library Materials, ANSI/NISO Z39.48-1992.
Manufactured in the United States of America.

To my niece, Dane'e

Contents

Foreword

Critical analyses of progressive education and its offspring (for example, the open classroom, constructivism, whole language) are rare but not new. In fact, one of the more interesting and unfortunate aspects of education in America is the tenacity of progressive education despite the critiques of Arthor Bestor, Dianne Ravitch, E. D. Hirsch Jr., Bonnie Grossen, John Stone, and others—who have exposed the murkiness of progressive "philosophy" and instructional design, the superficiality of progressive curricula, and, for many students, the destructive effects of progressive instruction.

Promise and Failure is an important book. It does not seek to marshal more evidence in an attack on progressivism. Rather, it answers the question: How does a set of moral ideals and reasonable curricular guidelines become transformed into a caricature of what its founders intended and then institutionalized in classrooms, textbooks, curricula, research, teacher training, and certification such that it is nearly impossible to change? In answering this question, Norris goes to the roots of progressivism in America and examines the ideas of Dewey and others. He then shows how these ideas were soon misinterpreted and taken to extremes, perhaps to serve certain ideological interests. As this (degraded) progressivism became doctrine in public schools and schools of education, its "truth" was no longer a subject of critical examination. Indeed, thorough indoctrination came to be the criteria that defined competence in classroom teaching and teacher training.

Let us hope that the gentle but insistent style of Norris's writing will secure an audience (even of progressive educators) who will be willing to examine progressive thinking and activities, and that the intelligence of his argument will lead to a true progressivism.

Martin Kozloff
June 8, 2003

Preface

I did not imagine a second book defending our profession would come about so quickly. The social sciences—particularly teaching and learning—continue to come under attack through a set of false dichotomies that present extremes (with no room for professional judgment) as the only hope for success. As such, our profession must be equipped with a body of literature that speaks the truth and defends the work that we do. Those of us who are knowledgeable in the social sciences continue to be amazed at how easily our profession is pushed far beyond the limits of common reason and how it is held to answer when the "reasonable" solutions don't work. It is difficult to imagine what Dewey might say were he alive today to see some of the very current gross misapplications of his life's work.

The practitioner/scholar brings a unique perspective to the issues and problems in the social sciences. It is quite common for those of us who work in colleges of education to have spent many years working in the field before moving into the ranks of academia. Consequently, our focus is not on researching and writing about the problems—essentially creating more data—but instead is focused on solving the problems. It is only through creating an awareness of the problems that resolution will ever come about. Much of what I discuss in this book comes from the general knowledge base. Likewise, much is from my two decades of experience as a public school teacher and choral director. If the writings of Dewey and other early progressive educators are ever to bring about positive change, the practitioner force cannot be "half-educated" in what progressive education means—and, most importantly, what it does not mean.

Throughout this book, the reader will find that I have admonished educational leaders for adopting an either-or, all-or-none mind-set when it comes to the design of programs for children. We know from the writings of John Dewey as well as our common sense that such a mind-set does not produce a better result, but instead produces exclusion.

There are a number of individuals and groups who contributed in many ways to the completion of this book. I must extend generous thanks to my colleagues in the College of Education at Nicholls State University for their support and encouragement in the completion of this manuscript. I must thank Dr. James A. Taylor, who has been an invaluable source of information and clarification on many issues. Dr. Lisa Lauer has been quite generous in sharing her expertise and experience. I extend thanks to Dr. Irvin Howard for his support and assistance, to Lee Gabala and Dr. Mary Mysing-Gabala for their encouragement and support, and to Mr. and Mrs. A. D. Geohegan III (and, of course, Nicholas) for their kindness, generosity, and encouragement in continuing this work. Dr. Barry Birnbaum has gently prodded me to complete the manuscript. My colleague and friend Dr. Angelle Johnson generously shared her research findings and expertise in middle-level education. My neighbor, friend, and colleague, Melinda Decker, has been helpful in bringing her perspective as a current practitioner in the public schools. My parents, A. C. and Mary Norris, have added a necessary perspective as they recalled and shared their experiences of being trained as teachers in the 1960s and having to unlearn much of that training over thirty years of work.

Although she may not realize such, my daughter, Sarah, has helped keep me focused in the completion of this manuscript. I'm glad she often asks what I'm writing about. I hope she understands.

Thanks are also due to Cindy Tursman, Acquisitions Editor for Scarecrow Press, for encouraging me to start another book so quickly. I must thank the Production Department of Scarecrow Press, particularly Associate Editor Jesse Goodman, for their prompt and efficient efforts to see the manuscript to print.

Introduction

Like teaching, psychotherapy can only work if the client makes it work. The importance of the client in processes of human improvement is the crucial one to discuss because although all the other professions that are involved in this kind of endeavor have the opportunity to pick their clients, teachers cannot.

—E. Wood, 1990

The verbiage of "progressive education" can elicit a number of responses from educated Americans (Semel and Sadovnik 1999). Some consider the ideals of progressive education to be the only conceivable answer to how we can best educate the youth of society (Kohn 1999). Others consider the mere existence of progressive education ideals to be entirely problematic for our schools (Grossen 1998). Such responses are contingent upon a number of things including, but not limited to, one's educational background, experiences, ideas, desires, wants, and expectations of what a quality of life is to provide. This opposing dichotomy of thought cannot be said to come about as a result of ill will or a desire to impugn. In the same manner in which any weather phenomenon is intended by nature to be "good," an individual's perception of this question is always intended to produce "good"—specifically, an education that is the best for all concerned. In schools, just as in the phenomenon of weather, it is an unfortunate corollary that too much of something that is supposedly good can be undesired at best or destructive at worst.

It is well known that an ignorant society cannot be self-sustaining and that the learned of society will always dominate the unlearned. Only those with a tyrant or terrorist attitude, or with the intent to oppress, would want a society of ignorant people. But despite what is considered to be the desired ideal, it would make sense that the person who has studied history, sociology, or the liberal arts—the less exact phenomena of mankind—will probably be more tolerant of ideas and methods of meeting goals that are less concrete than would the person who has studied the more exact sciences or business. Because education covers both the exact and less exact sciences, I discuss in this book the difficulties that are inherent in attempting to educate the youth of a democratic society.

Anyone who knows anything about American schools will assert two very common pieces of folk wisdom that are discussed ad nauseum in academic circles. First, there is not nor has there ever been a clear consensus on exactly what the schools are supposed to do (Postman and Weingartner 1973; Gay 1986; Wood 1990) and that everyone seems to have a "best answer" on how to run things (Hunter 1985). For over 100 years, American schools have fought a virtually unwinnable battle (Johnson et al. 1999), described by Postman and Weingartner (1973) as wanting "to know what the hollering is about." It has long been my argument and position that practically every educational squabble for the last century has not been a question of what works, but instead has been a question of extremes in ideology—traditional or essential (teacher centered, content) as opposed to progressive (learner centered, process). It has also long been my argument that—despite the success or failure of the extremes in ideological manifestations—teachers have only done as they were asked (Norris 2002). From both empirical and descriptive perspectives, there can be no question that the progressive ideology dominates all that happens in our schools, but not without having to fight for its rightful place. From primary school to postdoctoral study, the progressive ideas (and varying spin-offs) are the driving force behind all that is said and done in contemporary American education (Carr 1998; Cunningham 2001). Just as it is well known that the art and music of a society reflect the cultures and mores of that society, what goes on in the realm of American education "both reflects and shapes existing social political and economic relations" (Weiner 2000, 212).

The second piece of common folk wisdom heard in casual conversation is how generally bad our schools are. I am not the only practitioner/ scholar who has argued for years that, despite the failings and shortcomings of a very imperfect system, our schools do successfully manage to educate far more than they fail to educate. In observing human behaviors, it is interesting—almost comical—to find that virtually all parents complain about the same behaviors of their children, virtually all spouses offer the same complaints about their partners, and virtually all educators complain about the same hardships in their business. Obviously, the common arguments and complaints about the processes and products of our educational system have been around for a long time. To illustrate my point, Adler (1939) makes the following complaint:

> Elementary education is devoid of discipline. The basic routines in language and mathematics have been dropped or corrupted. Memory is not cultivated. Social studies, current events, manual arts and game occupy the major time. Secondary or collegiate education fails even more, though in part the failure is due to the inadequate preparation given in the elementary schools. Our Bachelors of Arts cannot read, write or speak their own language well; neither they nor, for that matter, our Masters of Arts, are acquainted with the liberal arts. They cannot read and they have not read the great books in all fields. They do not possess the leading ideas or understand the basic problems which are permanently human. They have been fed for years on textbooks and lecture courses which hand out predigested materials; and, as a result, they are chaotically informed and viciously indoctrinated with the local prejudices of professors and their textbooks. As a final consequence, education at the graduate and professional level has been necessarily debased. Law schools must teach reading; graduate schools struggle to get Ph.D. candidates to write simple, clear English. (144–45)

This passage certainly calls to question whether the "good old days" were as good as most of us would like to believe.

The progressive ideology is so deeply entrenched in the American idea of schooling that no one can imagine a desirable idea of schools as offering any other philosophy (Hirsch 1996). In recent years, there have been a number of scholars of curriculum and educational leadership who have upset the status quo in mainstream teacher education circles. Such scholars have begun to publicly call to question if the dominance of the progressive ideas that are not producing desired gains because the practitioner force is not "doing it correctly" or if the ideology is flawed and, as such, can never be made to work "correctly." It is unfortunate that such thinking today is generally dismissed as radical, old, uninformed, or not in the best interest of children. A practitioner in schools today who questions or fails to embrace the ideals that are hailed as progressive or forward-thinking will likely find himself considered a nonconformist, not a team player, and unwilling to "grow professionally." While I certainly do not consider myself to be an "antiprogressive" practitioner, I find it alarming how much progressive ideology flows through all efforts related to educational development or reform, teacher licensing, and school accreditation to the virtual exclusion of any other. We should all find it interesting that among educational leaders, professional growth is typically considered further exploration into progressive ideas and practices, generally culminating in some think-tank type of effort to further the cause of progressive education. For reasons that elude many of us, any exploration into more traditional practices, whether or not such may provide viable alternatives, is frowned upon.

As a veteran educator, teacher educator, and university professor for more than twenty years, and now as the parent of a teenage daughter, I have never been a nonbeliever in progressive ideals but have always been leery of their dominance, which virtually excludes any other possibilities. The discrepancies in the ideology only came to haunt me a few years ago as a graduate student when I became all too acutely aware of the fact that other ideas do exist that are real, viable, and possibly the more desired for the right population. I realized that such ideas are not inherently "wrong" simply because they are in contradiction to what is all too blindly accepted as what can only be the desired. I began to question what had been handed to me for so many years as the unerring gospel according to educational experts and began to see patterns of behavior in similar school systems. Further study revealed to me that although the progressive ideologies are the dominant force throughout all areas of teaching and learning, the inherent outcomes of progressive practices are often not what the public typically demands (Stone 2000a). It is disturbing to see public policy involving teaching and assessment that demand the tenets and ideals of progressive education, yet these demands (of teaching and assessment) so flagrantly contradict each other. We clearly have a public that is very ill informed and a cadre of educational leaders who are well intentioned but most certainly are unclear as to what they are asking the schools to do.

In this book we explore five areas. In chapter 1, we delve into the question of "what is progressive education?" Like many other educational phenomena, practices are based upon an idea, not vice-versa. The chapter explores ideas about progressive education. We see what progressive education is and is not.

In chapter 2, we briefly explore the origins of progressive education in this country. The time that such ideas began to surface over 100 years ago has been marked and remembered by serious controversy that was directly linked to a massive and unexpected growth in society. Much of the beginnings of progressive education can be traced to several select universities and school systems in the northeastern part of the country. Unfortunately, the work of certain individuals has been quoted, requoted, misquoted, and repeated so often that much of what is told is really a significant distance away from the original thinking.

In chapter 3 we explore some current practices operating under the claims of "progressive education." We look at and analyze the practices of some school systems relative to the true tenets of progressive education. We look at several very influential governing agencies whose ideals are noticeably skewed to the progressive with no consideration for any other. It is of great concern to social science scholars how frequently we see school districts and individual schools engaged in practices and methods that are claimed to be "progressive" when such practices are far removed from what was intended by the early theorists.

In chapter 4 we analyze why the supposed claims of the superiority of progressive education have failed. We examine various societal and sociological phenomena that progressive education has always claimed to "fix." The idea of schools (and progressive education) as a tool for social reform is explored as social problems of a century ago are compared to those of today.

In chapter 5 we discuss at length what must happen if progressive education is to survive and perform as promised. Progressive education, like quality parenting, is an idea that is made manifest by certain practices that support the idea while the real measurement of quality is the final outcome. In good teaching, just as in good parenting, the true results are usually not seen for some time—often for many years. Our society is too focused on immediacy and daily survival to allow the real time needed to see if what was done was done well. As civilized as we may be, we humans do inherently possess a mean streak. As such, good teaching, like good parenting, is a very inexact science and will always be subject to scrutiny by those who are convinced they could have done it better.

An ill-informed or half-educated leadership is dangerous to the main-stream population and particularly frustrating to those in the population who go beyond the half-educated status. It truly is my intent to defend progressive education; therefore, the reader should not assume that I am an opponent of progressive education. I am opposed to ill-informed educational leaders and policymakers using a small piece of a bigger idea in ways that are inconsistent with the intent and ideology. Likewise, I am opposed to leaders and policymakers trying to force a match between theory and practice when such a link does not actually exist or when the link is clearly not appropriate. In two decades of working in and around schools, I have observed some hideous discrepancies between ideas and practice that were not mean-spirited or ill-intentioned, but were the direct result of leaders and policymakers who simply did not know the truth. As a veteran teacher and trainer of teachers and administrators, I consider an "all-or-nothing" attitude to be both naïve and dangerous. Hampel (1999) states:

> Without frank, collegial discussion of the reform ideas, teachers are prone to stress part of a concept and overlook or reject the rest. For example, the popular "less is more" aphorism is often oversimplified. It is easy to envision "less" but much harder to see how less can be more. How can one Shakespeare play possibly offer more than three? Doesn't the state test require coverage, not depth? Won't our students botch the Advanced Placement exams? Without conversation and discussion, each question can become an exclamation point, an easy excuse to reject less-is-more. A major challenge for school reformers is to take away the easy excuses (especially the popular "But we already do that!") without insulting anyone. (45)

In 1946 George Orwell published the controversial book *Animal Farm* in which he used animal analogies to demonstrate how quickly and easily society can go from democracy to dictatorship when the constituents of society are not educated. It can be said that the ideas behind progressive education are intended to see that society does not reach the level described by Orwell. It is a dangerous and precarious situation for society at large, and certainly for school districts, when leadership pushes a specific agenda via bastardizations of complex ideas while keeping the workers ignorant of the ideas as a whole. We will see as we explore many practices that are claimed to be "progressive" or "based in research" that much of what goes on in school systems closely parallels what came about on the mythical Animal Farm.

**The Southwestern College Women's History Month Committee
Presents**

African American Women and Men: Where We Stand
Wednesday, February 27th, 2008
6:00pm-8:00pm

Leaders in education and local organizations discuss current issues facing African Americans, specifically in the areas of education, professional careers, and the family.

Speakers:

Panel Chair
> **La'Var Watkins**, Educator in Post Secondary, Adult Education, and Training and Development

Family
> **Pat Washington, Ph.D.,** President of the San Diego Democratic Women's Club
> **Monica Honore'**
> **Clovis Honore'**

Education
> **Angela Kinlaw**, Dean of Students at the School of Community Health and Medical Practices (CHAMPs) at the Crawford Educational Complex, and Founding Member of The BIG Saturday
> **Robert Hill**, Director EOPS at SWC

Business
> **James Henry**, Professor of Commercial Music
> **Karimah Lamar Rush**, Attorney

* Audience members are encouraged to participate in the discussion session that follows. Refreshments will be served.

Although some theories may be inherently flawed from the outset, it is generally accepted that there is no such thing as a bad theory. It is sometimes said that a theory does not go directly into practice—it must first go through people. This book is intended to discuss and defend the tenets and ideas of progressive education and assert most emphatically that progressive education has not failed the people, but that indeed the reverse is true (Radest 1983). An old piece of folk wisdom says "a little education can be a dangerous and destructive thing." This has unquestionably been the case with the implementation of the ideas and philosophies of John Dewey and the tenets of progressive education in the last century.

Chapter One

What Is Progressive Education?

Progressive School Director: The finest educational minds in this country
happen to be on our side.
Reverend Mother: God is on ours.

—Rosalind Russell in *The Trouble with Angels*, 1966

To truly appreciate the above citation, one would need to have seen the 1960s film *The Trouble with Angels* starring Rosalind Russell and Hayley Mills. In the film, Russell portrays the stern Reverend Mother in charge of both a convent and all-girl's school, and a staunch believer in traditional values who is fighting the liberal 1960s ideals. In the scene where the Reverend Mother confronts the director of the "New Trends Progressive School," each criticizes the ideals and methods of the other, clearly convinced that their ideas are "correct." This fictional scenario beautifully portrays the basis of this book.

A DESCRIPTION OF PROGRESSIVE EDUCATION

If we were to gather 100 of the brightest educational minds in this country and ask the question "What is progressive education?" we might very likely get more than 100 different definitions, probably none of which could be considered necessarily right or wrong. For some, the idea of progressive education consists of a collection of specific and observable activities and practices that are accepted by others who believe as they do. For some, progressive education is simply the rejection of any traditionally held notions of what school is, is about, or is supposed to do, or the rejection of anything related to the concept of the common school (Nadler 1998). For some, however, the idea manifests itself through a collection of ideas, or pieces of a philosophy, that are interpreted through modes of instructional delivery. For some, progressive education is "a multi-faceted movement aimed at changing school practices" (Englund 2000, 306). For some, it is simply an idea that is open to interpretation in a number of ways. None of these ideas are inherently correct or incorrect. Because of the inexactness of teaching and learning, it cannot be generically stated that either traditional or progressive ideas produce a better-desired outcome except in the context of what you are trying to achieve. There is good data to assert that teacher attitudes and beliefs tend to fall into one extreme or the other (Adwere-Boamah, Delay, and Jones 1982). However, the two are not necessarily opposing dichotomies or opposite extremes of the same idea.

For others, however, the idea is focused on the reasons for instructional design and delivery. Meier (2000) makes the following comparison:

> The tough part is that to some extent each of these ways is often espoused by some of the same people, and teachers and citizens alike are led to believe that both can be carried out simultaneously. . . . The kinds of schools they'd both probably like to see are, indeed, in some ways quite similar, with a focus on critical inquiry, curriculum depth, and collaboration and a downplaying of multiple-choice testing, rote memorization, and highly competitive classrooms. . . . What they disagree about is how to get there, and as a corollary to this, what must be sacrificed for "later" in order to get there "sooner." . . . Despite their often complementary intentions, these two ways stand in chilling contrast to each other. (179)

But from a slightly different perspective, Egan (1999) offers the following:

> What are the ideas that make up progressivism? The central belief—the most fundamental tenet of progressivism—is that to educate children effectively it is vital to attend to the nature of the child, and particularly to their mode of learning and stages of development, and to accommodate educational practice to what we can discover about these. The fact that this belief is almost universally shared among educators today supports Cremin's observation about how widely progressivism's tenets have become the conventional wisdom of American education, and Western education generally. (9–10)

Offering a "both sides of the question" perspective, Bernardo (1997) says,

As we have seen, then, what we have are two opposing approaches to education, one stressing knowledge that is demanding and challenging and academically rich content, the other stressing social growth, sensitivity, feelings, emotions, values, behavior, the fostering of self-esteem, and desirable attitudes toward life and learning which will lead to "self-directed" learners who are creative and productive. One side is learning and teacher-centered, the other student and group-centered. It is therefore natural that neither side will agree with the other side's system of testing. The progressives mistrust standardized tests, the traditionalists mistrust performance testing. This explains why progressives refuse to acknowledge that American schools are being dumbed down. For them scores from standardized tests tell less than half the story. It is what students can DO [emphasis in original] that matters. And the best measures of this are portfolios containing student work over a long period of time, and student projects. (7)

But in a more holistic sense, Partington (1987) says the following:

I take "progressivism" in education in a rather broad sense to mean the idea that desirable ends in education are both identifiable and capable of being, if not fully realized, at least more nearly attained than in the past or in the present. I place the many groups or individuals who fall within this wide definition of "progressives" into four main divisions. (5)

Halasz (1990) recalls her childhood experiences and memories of the transition from "traditional" to "progressive" schools. She states,

I think it was my mother who told me that North Country School, to which she was sending me in the autumn of 1942, was "progressive." That meant progressive had to be a glamorous, advanced, and positive thing. . . . Progressive education, it seemed, meant children being allowed to wear casual, practical clothes. At the Brearly School, which I'd been attending in Manhattan, I had worn frilly frocks. At North Country School, which was in the country in upstate New York, I wore blue jeans and lumberjack shirts. In New York, I took a bath every night; at North Country, two a week. In New York, Mrs. Johnson, the cook who looked after me, used to force my hair into corkscrew curls with the aid of metal curlers. At North Country, my hair hung straight, confined by one barrette. . . . In other ways, "progressive education" at North Country defined itself by the life we led, and a busy life it was. (104)

Partington (1987) describes what he calls "child-centered progressives"—
an area into which many varying ideas fall and differ but not necessarily disagree on the end result. He states that,

> Each distinctive child-centered educational theory possesses its own spe-
> cific recommendations; but none of them is willing to admit that its own
> theories are highly prescriptive. Typically they have appealed to allegedly
> scientific or natural laws, which once clearly discerned, would enable the
> progressive educator to realize in a non-interventionist way the inner po-
> tentialities of each child. (5)

In other words, while the progressivist camps that call themselves "child-
centered" may all have the same motives, none is quite willing to acquiesce to the fact that progressivism remains an idea, not a series of practices, and as such, there will be no particularly correct right or wrong way.
When Partington refers to the "radical progressives," he is speaking generally of those individuals who are in favor of massive expansion reforms
that are intended to bring a quality of "useful" education to the masses.
Partington argues that progressives from this camp find it difficult "to
evaluate the results of the changes they succeeded in promoting" (8).

Partington continues to categorize the progressive ideologies, referring
to the "instrumental progressives." This progressive camp sees its mission
as making the schools responsive to the "main needs of current Western societies" (13). This fits nicely with the ideological camp of the schools as
the tool for social reform and the betterment of society through creating an
educated population. But those progressives whom Partington classifies as
"liberal progressives" bring forth the question of which level and quality of
education is the most valuable. In view of the lack of consensus as to which
knowledge is of most value, it would almost seem an oxymoron to call
such an ideology "liberal." But perhaps the title of liberal does fit, in that
it refers to all ideas with respect to what is educationally important.

In a similar mind-set, Englund (2000) states:

> Progressivism is a multi-faceted movement aimed at changing school prac-
> tice. In addition to Dewey's ideas, the progressive movement advocated
> such specific curriculum methods as the project method of W. H. Kilpatrick
> while the child study movement, which appeared in many countries, was an
> offshoot of Progressivism. But many of these movements, and especially

the child study movement, were heavily criticized by Dewey. Progressivist educational movements have also been heavily criticized from totally different angles, and during the 1950's progressivism became discredited, except perhaps in the UK, partly as a result of the attack from such traditionalist educational philosophies as essentialism and perennialism, which arose to meet the challenge from progressivism. Dewey himself, in this struggle for the American curriculum, "hover[ed] over the struggle rather than belonging to any particular side" (Kliebard, 1986). During the restructuration years of the 1980's, progressivist ideas were rejected politically and traditional schooling restored (Telhaug, 1990). (306)

Walker (1981) offers a definition of progressive education that advocates the following six elements:

1. Education that is "child-centered." Although the terminology means different things to different people, it is safe to assert that Walker means the needs of the child supersede any other consideration;
2. The idea that children all possess certain natural tendencies that contribute to their ability to learn;
3. Children must have the autonomy to grow naturally;
4. The inherent ability in children to learn naturally correlates nicely with the idea of creativity;
5. Learning does not occur until the learner is ready to learn;
6. Legitimate curriculum can and is somehow linked to the natural curiosity of children.

Regardless of the perspective, throughout the vast amount of literature on progressive education, several common ideas continue to surface. Whether the perspective being supported is one concerning the "collection of activities" mind-set or the "ideas supported by practices" mind-set, we tend to find several common components. These components surface in the literature to varying degrees and are summarized here, but not in any particular order of importance, frequency, or desirability:

1. Some say, and apparently most believe, that the ideas upon which the tenets of progressive education is founded are directly attributable to John Dewey and his work that began at the University of Chicago just prior to the turn of the twentieth century.

2. As it is discussed and practiced today, progressive education rejects most of what is perceived as traditional or classical subject matter, method, or purpose of education.

3. Progressive education is an educational theory that is focused on the needs of the child, the complexities of children's physical and emotional growth, and the total development of the child. This idea is often summed up in a number of ways but most often as "educating the total child" or the idea of education as "child-centered."

4. Progressive education is focused on the development of generic problem-solving "life-skills," presumably in opposition to education that is focused on a body of common content. The literature is replete with extremist references to the idea that individual learning skills will create an individual capable of learning whatever they may choose or need to learn, causing the teaching of factual information to be superfluous and redundant.

5. Progressive education is focused on the practical and the application in opposition to the theoretical and the academic. Subject matter is not presented in separate disciplines but in a format whereby sciences and liberal arts areas are integrated and taught through natural life situations.

6. Progressive education is designed around the idea of the school as a theoretical cross-sectional model of society in which everyone is able to succeed in his or her own way, by some particular definition of success. As such, the work of the schools is not about creating uniformity among the masses, but instead about developing individuality within the masses. Therefore, the school is essentially the primary tool for social change.

7. Education is considered most effective and desirable when it can be perceived as democratic. This includes the design and delivery of systems of education in a democratic manner that likewise supports the ideals, mores, and values of a democratic society.

Throughout this chapter we discuss how the previous common components relative to progressive education are verbalized, elaborated upon, and made manifest among practicing educators. Wherever the concept of progressive education exists, we find some common ideas, attributes, and practices that are assumed present and necessary. We also find very terse arguments over whose idea is "right."

John Dewey

Much of what is touted as progressive education is traced to the writings and philosophical expressions of John Dewey. In the next chapter of this book we explore the work and writing of Dewey in more detail. For our purposes here, let us understand that Dewey is credited, fairly or unfairly, with what is frequently termed the progressive education movement in this country. Many writers who have studied Dewey to a level and extent beyond that of the average educator express concern about ideas that are erroneously attributed to Dewey. Kaplan (1997) states, "Although there is often a tendency to conflate Dewey's ideas with progressive education, Dewey himself argued that the distinction between traditional and progressive education is not particularly meaningful: what really matters is the vision of society and the possibilities for action that an education embodies" (433).

Similarly, Kesson (1999) makes the following comment:

Conservative critics of Dewey like to blame him for much of what they claim is wrong with our schools, including students' lack of discipline and respect for authority, teachers' emphasis on activity at the expense of learning, and the "dumbing down" of the curriculum. A careful reading of *Experience and Education*, however, reveals that if anyone is to blame for these problems, it's not Dewey but rather those who have misunderstood and misapplied his ideas. Indeed, Dewey wrote *Experience and Education* to address popular misunderstandings of his ideas and writings. He criticizes, for example, those educators who emphasize student freedom over learning. One discovers in these pages that Dewey was not an ideologue promoting any sort of "ism"—including progressivism—but rather a serious thinker seeking to provide a solid basis for teaching and learning. (73)

Donovan (1951), a Catholic educator in the 1950s, made the following comments:

One of the principles that are doing as much as anything else to undermine American schools is the fixed notion that education has to be fun. We won't have our children subjected to anything hard or bothersome. We have practically adopted a national education motto: "If it isn't easy, it isn't educational." . . . Among the more formal influences encouraging educators in their soft pedagogy is the educational theory of John Dewey. . . . Dewey, influenced by his early Hegelianism, declared war on all dualisms. . . . One of the dichotomies Dewey attacked was that between work and play. Unhappy about this opposition, he argued that given the proper setting (note the environmentalism), work should become play. Naturally he applied this notion to schooling and concluded that in a healthy educational environment, where children are engaged in matters of vital interest to them personally, the spirit of play will prevail. No doubt Dewey did not mean this to be taken as sentimentally as it has been by so many of his followers, but certainly his doctrine is a main prop, though not the only prop, supporting the "play way" in American education. (121)

In discussing experiences working in the newly developing progressive ideals, Rowland (1951), an experienced educator in the 1950s, made the following comments:

Progressive education is based on some false assumptions. It assumes that all boys and girls can be entertained to a point where they will be interested in all subjects. This is untrue. . . . The old-fashioned theory that the student should study what he needs to know rather than what interests him is sounder than the new theory. . . . Progressive education which overemphasizes "learn by doing" and underemphasizes "learn by thinking, reading and writing" is turning out men and women who are not leader material. Its products are not thinking men. (37)

Clearly, those in positions of leadership who espouse to be "progressive educators" really need a strong understanding of who Dewey was, what he stood for, and how he intended for his ideals to influence the education of the youth of our changing society. John Dewey was not a teacher but instead was a theorist. In the rhetoric surrounding his prolific lifetime of writing, people often forget that it was only for about seven years that he was actually around schools and children. After that time, he simply wrote, taught at the university, and basically startled the world by calling many traditionally held beliefs and practices into question. He was a pioneer of educational and democratic thought to the extent that more than fifty years after his death, the educated sector of America is still not sure what to do with his work. The arguments are endless.

It is human nature to want to belong, to conform, or to align oneself with a particular ideology. Humans seek comfort by surrounding themselves with others like themselves. As such, we humans generally tend to align ourselves with the ideology that not only makes us comfortable but that which is well received by others and creates a sense of community. In the effort by educators to align themselves with what is commonly perceived or believed to be the teaching of Dewey, Mirochnik (2003) states,

> Many of the teachers that I know find it most useful to ally themselves with theorists, whose notions about what should and shouldn't be done in the classroom fits well with their own notions of "good" educational practice. Today, many theorists present themselves as champions of the child, explicitly or secretly, derive their ideas from John Dewey, who spent most of his life urging teachers to abandon, once and for all, the ancient definition of knowledge as a pure, external, preexisting thing that, like truth, awaits discovery, and replaces it with the understanding that knowledge is made, not found. (73)

Throughout this book it will be argued many times that Dewey's ideas were quite frequently misunderstood, therefore causing gross exaggerations in practice. Burnett (1979) states, "The general conclusions I draw are that Dewey's educational philosophy seldom was applied, seldom was understood. Its confusion with romantic progressivism still abounds, and that intellectually inchoate congeries of ideas is both significant cause and effect of educational drift" (203).

Rejecting the Traditional

It is of concern to many writers that when observing what is supposedly progressive education in practice, we tend to find extremes in desirable ideas grasped and virtually exploited rather than an embracing of a balance. It is not unfair to assert that ideas taken to one extreme are often, if not usually, not a response to a well-thought-out plan of action or long-term goal but instead are a reaction to an opposing school of thought having been taken to an equal extreme. This idea seems to dominate through the belief that only through the "new" can the masses be served. It is sometimes assumed that any idea or practice remotely tied to the traditional cannot possibly serve the masses.

It is an unfortunate but very real phenomenon that the education business is marked by what seem to be years of reactionary extremes. In our business, the public is seldom willing to wait for results so that problems can be addressed in some sort of rational, systematic manner. We are willing to wait years for roads to be built, but not our schools. Consequently, much of what is touted as "reform" is little more than running to the "other side." When one school of thought doesn't like an idea, the reaction is to push for the opposite extreme with no consideration of a balanced perspective.

Educating the Total Child

In progressive education we generally find the idea of children before content, or more specifically, meeting children's needs before the advancement of an academic discipline. Hence, the verbiage of "child-centered" and "learner-centered" are seen quite often in the literature on progressive education and heard quite often where progressive education is practiced. Unfortunately, in the real practice in real schools, this terminology is often interpreted to extremes that are not within the scope of the idea or, in my experience, even to such extremes as to be ridiculous. In the purest sense, progressive education is based on the idea that the child is a complex individual (physical, emotional, intellectual, spiritual) with particular needs, strengths, and weaknesses. As such, the education of children should be designed and developed in a manner that concurrently addresses each of these aspects of the child.

But the idea of educating the total child becomes far more complex than many people realize. In recent years there has been a resurgence of popularity surrounding what is essentially an old African proverb: "It takes a village to raise a child." Former First Lady and noted child advocate Hillary Rodham Clinton wrote a book by that title that has stirred some controversy among conservative-thinking politicians, many of whom have publicly made remarks that clearly show their lack of understanding on social issues. The philosophical thinking here is that no person can live in total isolation from the rest of society and that everything about our individual personalities is a direct reflection of our lifetime of experiences. Additionally, society can only expect children to grow and live in the manner for which the groundwork has been laid. As an example, several years ago I heard a brilliant physician speak on the weak links of the society we have created that essentially create angry children. According to this individual, it should not surprise anyone to see angry children when they have come to realize by about the age of six or eight years that our society is quite dual in nature, and on which side of the duality they have fallen.

The progressive idea of educating the whole child falls nicely into the democratic ideals espoused by Dewey. It certainly makes sense that all aspects of the child must be nurtured so that the optimal societal tendency is togetherness, not divisiveness.

Critical Thinking/Problem Solving

In the concept of progressive education, the idea of critical thinking and independent learning is paramount. Although not necessarily attributable to Dewey, in the view of many educational leaders of today, the purest sense of progressive education tends to reject the teaching of a specific body of content in exchange for the teaching of a theoretical set of very generic problem-solving skills. This mind-set encompasses the idea that armed with such skills, students will become lifelong independent learners, able to learn anything they should choose to learn or need to learn as the need presents itself. Such generic skills are thought to produce independent citizens capable of making decisions that ultimately contribute to the betterment of self, family, and society.

But this is still only half of the story. Those who espouse the critical-thinking/problem-solving ideology generally think in terms of problems to be solved as real-life problems—avoiding the idea of teaching isolated skills that are later transferred to real-life situations. We will discuss this further in a later chapter.

Integrated Subject Matter

In the purest sense, the philosophy of progressive education rejects the idea of separate academic areas in favor of all academic content—the pure or natural sciences, social or behavioral sciences, humanities, literary or expressive arts—being presented and taught in an integrated format, each overlapping the other much like a large Venn diagram. Like any other argument in the traditional/progressive dichotomy, the ideology only becomes problematic when it is made so.

It is often argued that in order for any society to communicate, the society must possess a common body of factual information. The philosophy of progressive education is presumably in opposition to the concept of a common body of information that consists of isolated parts that are unrelated to one another. In the early days of the progressive movement, the idea was that by making the classical curriculum and the practical work efforts inclusive, the student would be "exposed" to some of the finer attributes of classical education and, as such, could conceivably be considered to hold a "well-rounded education." Since the working-class people were not likely to engage in conversation and discourse at that level, and would likely not care to study to be teachers, then a less-intense exposure to the classical elements of curriculum would be sufficient. Again, this is only part of the idea. In real life one must be able to read to be able to do most things. One does not read in one place, write in another, and perform mathematical calculations in another. The progressive ideology is intended to create a natural link between what some people call "school work" and "real work" or between "school life" and "real life."

Schools as the Tool of Social Reform

The philosophy of progressive education rejects the idea of creating uniformity among the masses via the teaching of a specific body of content. Instead, the uniformity that progressive education strives to create is one in which every member of society succeeds to the best of his or her ability by having capitalized on the strengths and weaknesses of each individual—a comparison that Hirsch (2001) would probably call "practical versus romantic." According to Weissglass (1999), the progressive ideology recognizes the American society as a quite imperfect, unjust entity. As such, students educated via progressive ideals will contribute to creating a more civil and democratic society. Progressive tenets strongly support the idea that an uneducated population cannot take care of itself or participate in democratic decision-making processes. An uneducated constituency can be neither self-sustaining nor function without the assistance of the system. Therefore, it is through education that society progresses for the betterment of all.

It is well known that the educated of society will always have advantages over the uneducated. At the same time, the old piece of folk wisdom that says "to get a good job, get a good education" is practically an oxymoron. In the working world of today, it is certainly not desirable, but not at all uncommon, to see college graduates working as hotel doormen, MBAs managing the night shift in a fast-food restaurant, or persons holding doctorates teaching elementary school. A high level of formal education does not necessarily align with what the economic climate of our country will support at any given time and the end result is that many in society are better educated than the economy can support (Levin 1981).

The idea of schools as a primary tool of social reform is often attributed to Dewey, but other controversial writers can share some of the credit as well. Even with the most beautifully conceived ideas, there will be imperfections and attributes that are open to discussion. Cohen (1998) explains the duality of Dewey's ideas:

> I have pointed out a central paradox in Dewey's ideas about schooling: on the one hand, he saw schools as an educationally useless and socially destructive expression of industrial capitalism, yet on the other, he was convinced they could be the central agency in reconstructing society. One might reasonably ask: If industrialism was so powerful as to be able to create these sad and damaging institutions, how could new curriculum and pedagogy turn them into agencies that would separate democracy in America from industrialism? . . . The paradox becomes even sharper as one pushes further into Dewey's view of educational reformation, for, while it would occur in schools, it was aimed at society. He wrote that his curriculum would enable schools to "affiliate . . . with life . . . [to] become the child's habitat, where he learns through directed living . . . [in] a miniature community, an embryonic society" (p. 18). These schools would be little communities whose "primary business . . . is to train children in cooperative and mutually helpful living; to foster in them the consciousness of mutual interdependence; and to help them practically in making the adjustments that will carry this spirit into overt deeds" (p. 117). (443–44)

Education as Democratic

In all the literature addressing the beginnings of the era and philosophies commonly referred to as "progressive," we consistently see a reference to the desire to align the schools and functions of the schools with the ideals of a democratic society. It is a generally accepted tenet of democratic processes that while it is not necessary for all involved to agree at all times, it is necessary for all involved to participate at all times—and participate meaningfully (Radcliff 1992). As such, formal education as a "democratic process" would be interpreted as education of the masses, not the select. As we delve into the idea of "education as democratic" or "education in a democracy," we see two very pronounced features. First, America seems to be the only civilized nation that has even attempted to create a system of education as such. Second, educating the youth in a democracy creates its own inherent set of problems because democracy is about the collective/masses whereas education is about the individual. Kaplan (1997) makes the following comparison:

> Democratic education is not just a matter of engaging young people in socially meaningful activity: the program must also include a reflective component that asks students to evaluate the purpose and meaning of their own activities. Even though adult-designed tasks may be of great social importance, and despite the fact that the opportunity to challenge existing power structures is undoubtedly invigorating, there is a crucial loss of democratic purpose at the very foundation of programs that pay no attention to the way in which such activities help students internalize the activism and connection of an adult agenda. The problem of democratic education is to develop programs and activities that honour, test and extend the student's *own* [emphasis in original] sense of commitment. . . . Democratic education succeeds when it aids students in establishing connections to community life. (433)

It is commonly known that a direct relationship exists between a person's level of formal education and the likelihood that the person will vote in local, state, or national elections. Certainly there are other intervening factors, but the most common link is the level of formal education. As such, Englund (2000) writes of the need for a balance between the ideals of participatory democracy—the idea that the effort and input of everyone is necessary for democracy to work—and that of a deliberative democratic perspective—the idea that citizens in a democracy can "agree to disagree" and live with certain compromises. Englund (2000) states,

> Like participatory democracy, deliberative democracy emphasizes participation in democratic processes, but it accentuates the character of the processes. Thus advocates of deliberative democracy stress the presence of different views or arguments, which are then negotiated, or put against each

other in argumentation. Two or more different views on a subject are proposed by persons who confront each other, but with an openness in the argumentation: "While acknowledging that we are destined to disagree, deliberative democracy also affirms that we are capable of deciding our common destiny on mutually acceptable terms" (Gutmann and Thompson, 1996: 361). Compared to participatory democracy, deliberative democracy especially emphasizes responsibility and consequences, implying that socialization to citizenship and the exercise of citizenship must be in focus. (311)

Teaching How to Think, Not What to Think

In modern practices that are called "progressive," we often hear reference to the idea stated above—that children in a democracy need to be taught how to think critically, see other points of view, and ask questions—not necessarily what they should think or that certain ideas, philosophies, or phenomena are inherently right or wrong (Gutmann and Thompson 1996). The premise behind the idea is that the acquisition of such general skills leads to the creation of individuals who are independent thinkers, capable of learning whatever they need to or want to learn. However, we will see in a subsequent chapter that this noble idea is often taken far beyond the bounds of common reason. But, at any rate, it can hardly be argued that a society that is trained to think can independently and collectively solve problems and will be a society in which fewer members are mistreated or otherwise oppressed.

Like many other well-intended precepts, this idea presents itself to a caring population as both a useful and humanitarian one, but on closer examination, is a near-false dichotomy because it is well known that critical thinking cannot happen without a body of information to support such thinking. The literate practitioner must not be deceived by the seeming simplicity of such ideals.

Teaching through Experiences, Projects, and Problems

We know that the purest form of progressive education, or at least as it is practiced today, rejects the idea of both a content-focused curriculum and any mode of instruction that may even remotely resemble tedium. The idea is often pushed that a number of critical skills and collections of skills can and should be taught through large projects that are creatively designed to encompass the necessary requisite skills. This idea links nicely with the concept of "thematic," as it is easy to design a project that can take large amounts of time to complete. But in dedicating the larger blocks of time, the teacher must be available to assist should the student encounter un-mastered requisite skills necessary for the completion of the project.

There is some controversy in current and early literature on the intent of the early progressive education writers and their ideas on project teaching, learning by doing, and so forth. Much of what has been practiced over the years as progressive education is often suspect by those who have studied Dewey and the early writings. Most scholars argue that it is an incorrect notion that a progressive curriculum is a series of projects (Tanner 1997). Gross (1989) offers many and varied reasons that a problems approach to curriculum has always been suspect and never really accepted, all of which seem to center around the part of human nature that is inherently resistant to change. He states,

> Although such great teachers of the distant past as Socrates and Abelard used a problem approach, it is largely recognized as rather new, with John Dewey's *How We Think* (1910) listed as the genesis. A by-product of the Progressive reform movement, it found itself at odds with dominant and traditional curricular organization and instructional approaches. Educational change moves very slowly, and the supposed recency of issue-centered programs has limited their acceptance. (185)

But even the best of ideas come with certain compromises both in concept and practice. Hirsch (2002) states,

> A theme in the literature of American education research is that natural, real-world simulations (hands-on projects), in which the student gains knowledge implicitly, are superior to the artificial, step-by-step methods of traditional schooling. It is initially plausible that exposure to the complex realities of reading—the "whole language" method—would lead to more sophisticated reading skills than stumbling along step by step with the bricks and mortar of the alphabetic code. The more general question is this, however: Should students be immersed right away in complex situations that simulate real life—the method of implicit learning—or should they first

be provided with explicit modes of instruction that are focused on small chunks deliberately isolated from the complexities of actual situations? (12)

All too frequently, academic conversation seems to miss the fact that many of the early progressive educators cautioned about ideas being taken to extremes. Concerning extremes in the project method, Bagley (1921) states,

> The present topic is approached, then, in an attitude that is about as far removed from dogmatism and "cocksureness" as it could possibly be. What we have specifically to ask concerning the project method may in the near future be recognized as quite beside the question. We are bound today to judge each new proposal by the standard with which we are familiar. But the development and acceptance of other standards may easily make our judgments of absolutely no consequence. (288)

False Ideas

As we read into the current literature on progressive education, there tends to appear a dichotomy of ideas that are at opposite extremes—an almost unfair battle being waged in which there apparently must be a winner. I often have to ask the question that if this battle were ever won (which, of course, it will not be), what would the winning side do? As the opposing sides are facing each other, we tend to find much of what sounds like political mudslinging just prior to a nasty election. We don't hear the merits of one side but instead hear the alleged problems and shortcomings of the other (Attwood and Seale-Collazo 2002). Desperate political candidates do not focus on their achievements, their ideas, or an approach to the issue or debate that is in the best interest of all concerned. Instead, these candidates call attention to one tiny piece of the opponent's record that, when told out of the context of entirety, calls the opponent's credibility into question. Hirsch (1997) describes this behavior in the following manner:

> Unfortunately, many of today's American educators paint traditional education as the archenemy of "humane" modern education. Even everyday classroom language unfairly pits the two alternatives against one another. Here are some typical descriptions used by progressives to compare old and new methods:
>
> Traditional vs. Modern
> Merely verbal vs. Hands-on

Premature vs. Developmentally appropriate
Fragmented vs. Integrated
Boring vs. Interesting
Lockstep vs. Individualized

Parents presented with such choices for their children's education would be unlikely to prefer traditional, merely verbal, premature, fragmented, boring, and lockstep instruction to instruction that is modern, hands-on, developmentally appropriate, integrated, interesting, and individualized. But of course this is a loaded and misleading contrast. (6)

There are some obviously flawed ideas present when we assume that there must be a winner in every ideological debate (Hillerich 1990). It is really sad and ignorant to see such opposing sides to a question that really has few boundaries. It is equally sad and ignorant to hear all the seemingly political rhetoric bash one side against another. Common sense coupled with Dewey's writings make it clear that progressive education is not supposed to be anti-intellectual, lacking in content knowledge, or focused on feelings rather than achievement. Hirsch (2000) nicely summarizes this argument: "In short, many progressive educational assertions that have attained the status of unquestioned fact by being repeated constantly are huge oversimplifications. They wither under close scrutiny. And they have done serious harm" (175–76).

But the question must go further. Is it possible that progressive education can work for everyone? When we read the early progressive literature and refer to "the masses," are we referring to every single person in society, or do we actually mean "most people"? We encounter the argument again and again that no particular system can be perfect or even adequate for everyone every time. The idea of perfectly serving everyone every time should be reexamined.

WHAT PROGRESSIVE EDUCATION IS NOT

In the fall of 1937, an article appeared that, while not particularly complimentary to the ideology of progressive education, has been cited over the years and probably has contributed significantly to the traditional/progressive squabble. Withers (1937) offered the following vignette:

A lady visited a progressive school. In the first classroom several boys were hitting each other with sticks and some were reeling around in a strange fashion. "Oh," cried the visitor, "these boys are hurting each other, and some of them are behaving as though they were drunk." The teacher calmly replied, "Of course, they are drunk and soon they will be sick. You see, they are studying the Whiskey Rebellion." After a moment's pause, the teacher continued. "Would you care to visit the class studying the *Murders of the Rue Morgue*"? (401)

Common sense would dictate that children would not have been allowed to become drunk at school, but it serves to illustrate the extremes in thought that have fueled this century-long battle.

It can hardly be argued that those of a civilized democratic society want all of society (meaning virtually everyone, not literally everyone) to possess the capability to participate meaningfully and continue the practice of democratic ideals. This would not be the desired ideal if one lived on Manor Farm, but it is the desired ideal in this country. But, despite the desirability of such ideals, general conversation among seemingly educated people tends to mistreat both the premise and the intent of what progressive education was intended to do (Pipho 2000). Let us examine some false notions about progressive education, the apparent origins of those false ideas, and what the literate practitioner should know in order to make the best decisions.

It is often argued by rather conservative thinkers that "progressive education is at the heart of all the problems in our schools." It is difficult to understand how such a general statement can really and truthfully describe the problems in the schools. Such arguments are little more than finger-pointing by the unknowing. It has to be remembered that the ideals of progressive education were and are intended to make a useful public education accessible to everyone, regardless of background, social status, or handicapping conditions. Knowledgeable, educated people have always known this and are not opposed to the ideology. They are opposed to the misapplication of the ideology. It would fall somewhere between somewhat naïve and outright stupid to ever assume that one idea, regardless of the nobility of intent, would be the answer to the monumental task of what our schools are trying to accomplish. In the same manner that it is naïve to assume that medical science will "fix" all the sick people of the world and do it perfectly every time, it is equally naïve to assume that the schools will ever be able to accomplish a comparable mission. Despite the generally argumentative nature and cyclical behavior of our nation's efforts at school reform, the schools do manage to successfully educate far more than they fail to educate.

It is hard to imagine the social science fiasco that would come about should the schools attempt to impose what is termed a "classical" education on all children, regardless of background, social status, or handicapping conditions. In the days when people of any formal education were given the "classical" education, basically two factors existed. First, it was generally the people of means who could afford the luxury of such. Most children after a certain age were forced to begin working to contribute to the family sustenance. Second, the people of old who were afforded a "classical" education usually did so primarily with the intent of furthering their education at the college level. There was a time in this country when most adults did not go to college. Today far more adults attend college or some sort of postsecondary education because the workforce and labor requirements demand such. Just as the learned of society came to realize about a hundred years ago that some other pressing needs were emerging relative to the education of the youth of society, the same is true today. In general, it simply is not fair to assert that the ideals of progressive education are to be blamed for the supposed failure of our schools. This supposed dismal failure is not supported by good evidence. There truly is not a valid link between the two.

It is often argued that progressive education and its processes are "anti-intellectual." This terminology and thought tends to stir very mixed professional feelings. There are rather traditional thinking people who often are quoted as referring to "anti-intellectual" as anything other than the memorization of various bodies of content and never delving any further. This is a very shortsighted perspective, and scholars of teaching and learning such as Hirsch (1996) and Alfie Kohn (1998) would argue to the contrary. A dictionary definition of "intellect" is "the ability to learn and reason; the capacity for knowledge and understanding." Progressive education is about the ability to learn and reason, and to acquire knowledge and understanding in order to become a functioning individual in a society of the masses. Except when progressive ideals are pushed far beyond the bounds of common sense and reason, can it ever be assumed that true progressive ideals—not those pushed to ridiculous extremes—are anything but intellectual?

Another common argument is that progressive education is "focused on feeling, not on content." Unfortunately, in view of the inherent individualistic nature of progressive ideals, there have been thinkers over the years who have pushed the ideas to a much greater extreme than many would consider logical. As such, there have been schools, school systems, educational leaders, and writers who have blatantly misinterpreted ideas and perspectives to include the idea that feelings were more important than academic content. In recent years some writers have published some rather scathing indictments of a system that tends to consider feelings of self-worth over academic growth (Stone and Clements 1998; Stout 2000; Sachs 1996). Most of us have witnessed the type of educational mind-set whereby educators are told that feeling good about oneself leads to success when we know clearly that any reputable research that has been done in this area strongly indicates the opposite to be true: self-esteem comes about from successful practices. It would appear from the writings and anecdotal observations that such problems are quite real in some places. But no one of any degree of intellectual honesty can truly argue that it is the progressive ideology alone that is responsible for such. The problem comes about when ideas are misapplied or used to support a particular agenda—the antithesis of intellectual honesty.

There is currently in this country a movement that recognizes and supports the developmental needs of the middle-school-aged adolescent. The middle school movement came about more than thirty years ago when educators and social scientists realized that the format of the traditional junior high school could no longer fulfill its mission. As such, the middle school ideology emphasizes an awareness of the developmental needs of the middle-school-aged child and the focus on child-centeredness—whatever we perceive that to be. Consequently, many unfairly relate "progressive" and "middle school" as some sort of educational wasteland whereby children are not taught any academic content, but instead are pampered to such extremes as to never develop the independence of thought necessary to function at the secondary level (Bradley 1998). We know that complicated ideas that are misunderstood lead to the creation of false dichotomies. The false dichotomy here is the question of some balance between real academic standards and the consideration of the child.

There is literature supporting the fact that real academic standards and the developmental needs of middle-school-aged adolescents can really mesh, and are not an "untenable dualism" (Anfara and Waks 2000, 50). The dualism here is hardly a two-sided issue, but another ideological battle that will forever be fought but never won. Anfara and Waks (2000) state,

> The emotive terms used to state the academic vs. developmental dualism (hard vs. soft, tough vs. tender, rigor vs. ease) bring to mind the image of a pendulum. "Reformers vacillate," Cuban (1990) noted, "between teacher-centered and student-centered instruction, academic and practical curricula" (p. 4) What keeps the pendulum swinging is the antithesis of two opposing value concepts, neither based on solid empirical ground, each appealing to certain groups. As Wise (1989) reminded us, "many of the proposed 'solutions' to current problems have little . . . empirical grounding" (p. 36). (47)

In recent years the field of math instruction has come under serious criticism as leaders in the field have attempted to make the study of mathematics more useful and appealing to today's generation of children. It is a frequent complaint among teachers that as each generation of children arrives at school having been more and more influenced by the visual media, it becomes more and more difficult to hold their attention. One colleague stated, "They think they should be entertained at school, not study." So, as happens frequently, a well-meaning attempt to make mathematics more useful, the boundaries between content and application have become a bit vague. Loveless (1997) says,

> The problem with this argument is that it's based on conjecture. We don't know if learning by osmosis really works, nor the long-term consequences of students failing to master basic skills. We don't know whether students who can't grasp, say, the equivalence of 0.25 and 25 percent actually go on to successfully learn calculus. Research has yet to document large numbers of students who fly through algebra but are clueless when it comes to fractions. Moreover, parents worry when their 5th graders can't multiply single-digit numbers without pocketfuls of beans and sticks. Teachers are concerned that the mastery of basic skills signifies something more than computational proficiency, that students who learn these facts to an automatic level also gain a deeper knowledge of mathematics, a sense of number unfathomable to those who don't know them. (2)

Chapter Two

Origins of Progressive Education

Educational reform is not a pass or fail phenomenon. Every reform effort contributes to the overall development and continuous improvement of the educational system. The educational community and the public learn from the experience. It is also the case that many hold the misconception that a particular reform will, once and for all time, fix our educational problems.

—R. W. Bybee, 1998

To those of us who qualify as veterans in the field of public education, it is almost amusing when we hear casual conversation lamenting the current status of public education in this country. Well-meaning comments such as "the good old days" and "getting back to basics" are practically loaded in the Freudian sense. The creation of the public schools in this country began in an effort to see what could be considered the "common school"—the school that everyone could attend and that would provide a level of education that would produce a relatively uniformly educated populace that could function socially and be self-sustaining. Generally, our society has produced such a system of public education although it would be naïve to ever assume or assert that such a system has ever been or ever will be perfect. It has taken a long time for our schools to reach the point where they are today. There is no question that any movement away from the current status will likewise take some time. The real question to be asked (that no one wants to ask) is how to go about moving away from the current status and do so in a reasonable and feasible manner that will benefit the masses with little discomfort.

The origins of the dominant ideas known as progressive education in this country are quite easy to trace because they did not begin in the schools. As we search to determine the origins of what we now call progressive education, several names of persons and institutions of higher education continue to surface. Likewise, certain terminologies continue to sporadically appear and reappear as different names to the same idea. And, unfortunately, the same arguments come forth over and over again, each time assuming there will be a winner—essentially the same behaviors we see in a bad marriage. But to understand the how and why of the progressive education movement, we must look at the social and political climate that has evolved with this country. Levin (1991) describes the status of our nation at that time:

> The Progressive Movement in American history encompassed the period from roughly the 1880's through the 1930's. Urbanization, coupled with the completion of America's westward expansion, stimulated private and governmental efforts to improve rather than just enlarge many social institutions and services. Labor activism, woman suffrage, child labor laws and settlement houses for the poor grew during this period. So did the nation's first attempt to transform the "common schools" vision of Horace Mann into mass elementary and secondary education for highly diverse and increasingly urban student populations. (72)

The drive for reform is an inherent part of the American experience. Likewise, it is a fact of life that movements in the social and behavioral sciences come about in response to the people's desire to bring about change. The unfortunate parallel to this fact is that we humans are attracted to that which is familiar and similar, thereby making us inherently resistant to change. Our nature, therefore, does little to support change for the sake of improvement. As we look into the origin of progressive education—the where, how, and why it all began—we must consider a number of things, including but not limited to, the social circumstances of the day, the manner in which society was growing and changing, and the idea behind the desired changes being sought. Sometimes in the noise of the battle between ideological extremes, we forget that the ideas came about from a sincere desire to improve society.

THE EMERGENCE OF PROGRESSIVE IDEOLOGY

The verbiage of "progressive" often evokes ideas of the schools, but the terminology and its relation to our nation's history is by no means related only to public education. During the time referred to as the Progressive Era— ranging from late 1800s to the early 1900s—the nation was making a shift from a farming economy to an industrial one, and new ideas about how best to serve the masses came into question. Our nation was a little over 100 years old and had grown considerably in many regards—particularly with the abolition of slavery—but with each passing year, the gap between those of wealth and prosperity and those without was growing wider. By the late 1880s, slavery was no longer legal in this country, but it was clear that the person in society who was at the greatest advantage was the white male who could read and write, and of course, who had the financial resources to support his desire to improve himself and life in general. At this time, essentially the only people in American society who were allowed to vote were white men.

Some of society were content to continue with the status quo, but others knew that a democratic society is difficult to sustain when extremes in material gain are prominent. As such, social reforms were needed to narrow the gap between wealth and poverty. Lincoln knew that simply declaring slavery illegal would not immediately improve the quality of life for former slaves and would create many unforeseen problems that would take years to correct. Likewise, these reformers had the foresight to know that a society full of poor and uneducated people, unable to support and sustain themselves, would be the downfall of society. It is a safe, generic assertion that the early progressive reformers, both political and educational, were focused on creating a society that could be perpetually self-sustaining.

Part of the problem blocking social reform of the time was not a great deal different than that blocking reform today. Humans are quite resistant to change and our nature causes us to migrate toward the familiar. Consequently, we find the more privileged of society talking about the deplorable discrepancies between social classes but unwilling to do much about them. The most effective work of the early activists surrounding the progressive movement in America brought about an awareness of the plight of the less fortunate.

But even within the boundaries of the progressive movement, there were discrepancies and differing points of view (Holt 1994). Levin (1991) said,

> The Progressive Education movement, particularly during the first three decades of this century, split into what may be viewed as two camps. The wing commonly called *child centered* was exemplified by the work of John Dewey. The other end of the Progressive continuum, considered here a *mass education* (sometimes called *administrative*), was exemplified by the rising "science" of educational testing led by E. L. Thorndike and colleagues at Columbia University and by the growth and centralized authority of large, bureaucratic school districts. (71, italics in original)

Although there are many arguments in this area, the terminology of "child-centered" is strongly attached to Dewey. The concept of "child-centered" will be discussed at length in chapter 4.

In any profession, there will be differing perspectives on the same question. Olson (1999a) discusses three differing schools of thought during the Progressive Era. First we saw the "pedagogical progressives"—those who were considered progressive by the manner in which they designed instruction. These were the thinkers who tended to prefer more loosely structured, less-formal teaching. In this school of thought, we find integrated curricula, much use of hands-on teaching, and teaching focused on the likes and interests of the children. Second, we saw the "reconstructionists"—sometimes called "social progressives" or "social reconstructionists." These thinkers tended to see the schools as the tool by which we would see the social order change as the level of education among the masses changed. Last, we saw the "administrative progressives"—those thinkers who sought to design schooling at various levels to accommodate the individual backgrounds and deficiencies that are inherently encountered when attempting to serve the masses. The relatively new science of mental testing and measurement played a conspicuous role in this school of thought.

Regardless of the social models made manifest by the behaviors of the various leaders in the early Progressive Era, one uncomfortable question would remain unanswered, even to this day. Would this humane and democratic mode of public education truly support the crux of the progressive movement—the question of education serving both the elite and the humble? Hlebowitsh and Wraga (1995) state,

Prior to the rise of progressivism, American schooling was wedded to a rote-and-recitation model that elevated the significance of purely academic learning pursuits. Progressive-experimentalists, in fact, were among the first to question this priority and to help shift the instructional orientation of the school away from the intellective tradition that was supported by the mental disciplinarians and toward the representation of school concerns and social activities in the curriculum. By seeking to cultivate the sociocivic function of schooling and the social service role of the educator, these progressives held to a strongly committed sense of advancing social reform through public education. . . . These very same progressives were also at the forefront of annihilating the belief that class division was a biologically grounded part of human nature and were united in unbraiding the tendency toward laissez-faire individualism in the industrial and financial sectors of the society. The effect was a widened sense of purpose for the school that included more than academic prowess or economic gain and that, as mentioned, marked a movement toward a more universal publicly supported school system. (8–9)

Among the writers who influenced the progressive movement and who were hailed by most educated readers was George S. Counts. In 1932 Counts released a controversial book entitled *Dare the Schools Build a New Social Order?* He did not see the schools moving forward but instead supporting the status quo in the delivery of services. Counts argued that the schools must not become a cross-sectional model of the existing societal structure, catering to the needs of the privileged while diminishing those of the less fortunate. Hlebowitsh and Wraga (1995) state,

To Counts, the problem with schooling had less to do with the institution of schooling itself than with the larger socioeconomic situation, which Counts described as an economic aristocracy. Without the reconstruction of the economic order, the school would always be a handmaiden to those who possess economic power. On this point, Counts projected his worst fears, stating that the maintenance of an economic elite would lead to differential forms of education constructed along class lines. In the resulting dual system, the children of the masses would attend lower and inferior schools suited for their presumed subordinate status. To avoid these perils, Counts reasoned that the schools would need to resist deliberately the domination of the economic aristocracy by revitalizing collectivist democratic causes and principles in the school. Since the controlling hand of economic oppression infused the school with the philosophy of economic individualism,

which fostered egoistic and competitive values in education, the schools
themselves, particularly the teachers, would need to defuse this power by
committing themselves to the doctrinal position of reordering the socioeconomic order toward a collectivist or workers' society. This kind of preset
commitment to a social arrangement put Counts on the periphery of exper-
imentalism, though it is not easy to dismiss him because, within the collectivist context, he did believe in the need for students to confront problematic situations in ways that developed their reflective powers. In fact, Childs
(1956) and Callahan (1971) have argued that Counts was a pragmatist in the
Deweyan tradition. (14–15)

To understand the progressive movement, we must look further and ask
some questions about how schools looked and functioned at the time. We
can see physical structures through photographs or artifacts that have survived, but teaching practices of the time are really only observable by a
limited number of surviving documents. Cuban (1983) cites the following:

At the turn of the century, the prevailing form of teaching was teacher-
centered. Clues about what went on in classrooms appeared in rows of
bolted-down desks, rooms designated as "recitation" at the high school, and
the omnipresence of textbooks in the published courses of study. . . . Generally classes were taught in a whole group. Teacher talk dominated verbal
expression during class time (64 percent of the time, according to Stevens).
Student movement in the classroom occurred only with the teacher's per-
mission, e.g. going to the chalkboard. Classroom activities clustered around
teacher lectures, questioning of students, and the class working on textbook
assignments. Uniformity in behavior was sought and reflected in classroom
after classroom with rows of desks facing the blackboard and teacher's
desk. (163)

But, according to Cuban (1983), by the 1920s and 30s, the picture was
somewhat different: "Recall that during these interwar years there was an
explosion of interest in the project method of teaching, joint teacher-
student planning, small group work, independent study, and curriculum
revision. Progressive ideology had become the conventional wisdom
among educators. But only a few of those ideas had penetrated classrooms" (163).

In any discussion of progressive ideals and democracy in society, politics, schools, or whatever, there is an aspect of the question that is seldom

approached. There are social science scholars who continue to raise the question whether the emergence of progressive ideologies have done—or were intended to do—the exact opposite of what most people believe. Katz (1971) argues that American schools have always been designed in such a fashion that the privileged of society are well served while the less fortunate have only been served to varying degrees. There are some who believe that reform efforts over the years have been a perpetual cycle of keeping the line quite visible between the haves and the have-nots (Generals 2000). Wilson (1991) and Coleman (1991) argue that creating an equal opportunity for formal education will not create the ability or the desire to pursue such. These writers generally support the notion that family background and social class are more strongly linked to school success than any circumstances that can be artificially created by political movement.

In an entirely different vein, Anderson (2000, 2002) argues that the progressive movement grew in relation to the Civil War and the abolition of slavery. Anderson (2002) states,

> To put it another way, the war ultimately ushered in the Progressivist era, progressivists being people who had a religious-like belief in the power of the central government. Inherent in Progressivism, of course, is the belief in rule of force. To put it another way, progressivists believed in the miraculous power of coercion, believe that if government could utter enough threats, people could do anything, including turn natural law upside down. (2)

Anderson (2002) goes on to argue that the influence of progressive ideals in society have hindered the common man's ability to do for himself, and have kept the less fortunate dependent on the state. He explains, "The typical picture of Progressivism as painted by leftists today is one of wise and benevolent intellectuals using the apparatus of the state to impose 'solutions' to 'protect' Americans from the ravages of capitalism and to spread American concepts of fairness and justice to the masses. Indeed, the results of Progressivism are almost opposite of what we are told" (4).

But of particular note is the assertion by Callahan (1981) that Dewey's idea of democracy is flawed. He argues that Dewey's idea of democracy has an underlying tenet of supporting the masses at the possible exclusion of the individual. Callahan (1981) states,

As one begins to explore the implications of Dewey's criterion of democracy, the most striking fact to emerge is the extraordinary emphasis he placed on the desirability of social solidarity. When he wrote of "shared interests" in a democracy he did not mean simply that members have interests in common but rather that they pursue these in a context of co-operative endeavor. Thus the fulfillment of the individual's interests is largely dependent on the action of others as well as his own; and so each stated interest becomes a cohesive force within society uniting human beings through the bonds of inter-dependence. These co-operatively pursued interests will be numerous, varied, and each will be shared by all, or by as many as possible, in a democracy; and an exceptionally high degree of social unity would obviously be ensured in this way. Philosophers in the liberal tradition have generally stressed the ethical importance of personal autonomy or independence, but Dewey explicitly endorsed personal dependence as a positive attribute. He saw it as one of the "powers" of childhood and noted that there is a danger that increased personal independence will decrease the individual's social capacity. In a democracy that danger is forestalled by creating massive personal inter-dependence. Solidarity will also be enhanced by the way in which common goals and purposes are pursued since this will undoubtedly be based on the intense allegiance to scientific method which all share. The stress on solidarity is again evident in the fact that democratic societies may enjoy full and free interaction with other groups since this will evidently ensure the partial integration of democratic communities into a larger whole. In short, Dewey's utopia is a world in which mankind has become one highly unified family through close communication, co-operative effort, common interests and an empiricist faith. (168)

PROMINENT INDIVIDUALS IN THE EARLY PROGRESSIVE EDUCATION MOVEMENT

As we look into the history of the progressive movement, there are specific names of persons and schools that remain static. This portion of the chapter examines several of those individuals and schools, the work that was done, and how that work is still quite influential today.

John Dewey

When I approached the publishing company about writing this book and described what I had in mind—both a defense and critique of progressive education—the editor said, "You mean progressive education—as in John Dewey?" This serves to illustrate my point that when we delve into the question of progressive education, the name that immediately comes to the minds of most people is John Dewey and, unfortunately, the late Dewey is often credited a bit unfairly (Olson 1999b). When a person is credited with being the catalyst of some mode of social change, it is usually helpful to understand the person's perspective or his background and experience that contributed to his desire to bring about social change. Dewey's upbringing was quite humble, having been raised "in rural Vermont and attended the tiny University of Vermont" (Zilversmit 1993, 3). According to Vandervoort (1983), "Dewey was deeply concerned about teaching practices that prevailed in America in the late 19th and early 20th centuries. He was disturbed by what he felt was elitism, irrelevance, and triviality of curricula in most schools, and denounced science educators who emphasized rote memorization and mechanical routine at the expense of inquiry and creativity" (38).

Dewey worked as a high school teacher for a short while and returned to Johns Hopkins University to earn a PhD. Following a short tenure at the University of Michigan, he accepted a position at the University of Chicago in 1894 (Zilversmit 1993). It was during his time at the University of Michigan that his thinking grew to include a general concern for elementary and secondary education (Vandervoort 1983). To fully understand the historical significance of Dewey's work originating at this relatively new university, we must first understand what was happening socially, politically, and economically that would allow new ideas to come to the surface.

At the turn of the century this country was in the midst of an industrial revolution. In the year 1894, slavery had only been abolished for some thirty years and the national economy that had previously been driven primarily by farming and plantation work was now moving to an economy supported by industry, primarily the production of steel (Olson 1999a). Families were moving from the farms to the cities to find work and the population of the cities was growing rapidly. According to Vandervoort (1983),

Dewey grew up in a nation recovering from the wounds of the Civil War. The scientific, social, and cultural changes that arose in Europe were reaching across the Atlantic to tug at the fabric of American tradition and character. These forces, coupled with a powerful drive toward industrialization,

wrought changes in all facets of American life. Some of the more en-
lightened colleges and universities were beginning to establish philosophies and curricula more in keeping with the times. Among these was the
University of Vermont, where Dewey matriculated in 1875 when he was
not quite 16. (39)

Many social scientists believe that it was during this time that the traditionally held perceptions of family and stereotypical gender roles began
to change. American life had typically been centered around the farming
lifestyle, which necessitated males accepting responsibility for some work
and females accepting responsibility for others. Families did not live as
we might assume a hermit might live, but due to the physical distance between farms, families did live a considerably more private and isolated
existence (Bly 1990). Family structures were tight, as everything about
life—the work and the fun—required the input and cooperative participation of everyone—the ideals espoused by democracy.

As fathers began to work in factories, the role the children had previously played—as "mentee by default"—could no longer exist. Children
could become part of the work and running of a farm whereas such could
not happen in factory work (Bly 1990). Prior to this time, any type of formal education for children had been the responsibility of the farming parent and, as such, teaching children to read and write was a hit-or-miss effort at best. The more affluent families could bring someone to the farm
to teach the children while the less affluent simply passed on whatever
they were able. As the city population began to grow, the question of some
sort of formal schooling for this massive influx of children, many who
would not have been able or even willing to attend school only a few years
earlier, was at the forefront (Eakin 2000). Kliebard (1985) states,

> It was in this context that Americans looked more and more to schools as a
> vehicle for addressing these problems. While the traditional humanist cur-
> riculum engendered some dissatisfaction during the 19th century, it
> nonetheless remained fairly stable, bolstered in large measure by the theory
> of mental discipline. When certain subjects, such as the classical languages,
> were criticized for being impractical or even useless, as was the case with
> the controversy over the Yale College curriculum in 1828, there was always
> recourse to a justification similar to that espoused by Plato; certain subjects
> had the power to develop the mind more than others, and development of

the various faculties of the mind, such as memory, reasoning and imagination, was the chief function of schooling. Thus, a combination of the humanistic ideal and a belief that powers of the mind needed to be trained through vigorous exercise helped support existing curricular practices. (33)

Obviously, working on the farm required very little reading, writing, and math skills beyond what was necessary for managing the farm, or perhaps the desire to read the Bible. Living in the urban areas greatly increased the need for a level of general literacy because of the increased dependence on trade and commerce and the need to communicate with people outside the rather isolated and focused culture of farming.

The writings that have survived until today by people who knew John Dewey indicate that all his life Dewey was a deep social thinker and believed in the empowerment of the people (Westhoff 1995)—or what Burnett (1988) would call "militant liberalism." Our country was in the midst of this revolution in societal mores and values, and undergoing changes that no one had quite expected. All along, Dewey had been laying his groundwork that was primarily to quietly bring about an awareness of the fact that since society was changing anyway, an educated society could quite naturally change for the better. So, the political and social timing was perfect. When Dewey arrived at the University of Chicago in 1894, he was a young professor with very little real-world experience to his credit, but he had a great interest in schools and had long believed that the schools were the link by which society would improve or fall. He had traveled some and had seen many of the European schools that were greatly influenced and designed around a very romantic idea of childhood and children's physical and cognitive development. Zilversmit (1993) says,

Even before he came to Chicago, Dewey was dissatisfied with a philosophy that treated ideas as abstractions, unrelated to daily living. He had been concerned with finding ways in which academic philosophy and psychology could play a larger role in dealing with broad social questions. He had begun to expand philosophical discussion by bringing social issues, such as the ethics of participating in a strike, into his classrooms (Coughlan, 1975). He argued that it is only "when philosophic ideas are . . . used as tools to point out the meaning of phases of social life" that "they begin to have some life and value" (Bernstein, 1966, pp. 31–32). Dewey's philosophy supported a new approach to the discipline, providing a link between the world of ideas and the social world. By the time he got to Chicago, Dewey had rejected philosophical idealism and developed a philosophical position that denied the separation between the spiritual world of thought and the ideals and the natural world of human action (Westbrook, 1991). (3)

Based upon his conviction that philosophy and theory were there to support mankind, he pushed the administration of the University of Chicago to develop a department of pedagogy that he would be allowed to codirect along with the department of philosophy. It appears that it was this administrative action that set his work in motion. He believed adamantly that most children did not need to be taught in the traditional manner whereby each child was taught absolutely the same thing in the same way. He rejected the idea that learning was necessarily tedious. Dewey believed that anything children were systematically taught should begin with the natural curiosity of children, thereby relinquishing the traditional fragmentation of curriculum and its delivery. But more than anything else, Dewey believed that systematic instruction could and should be a democratic process that would contribute to the furthering of a democratic society.

William Heard Kilpatrick

William Heard Kilpatrick is recognized as a prominent figure in the progressive movement, primarily due to his writings on the "project" method—the idea that children are best taught through problem-solving types of projects that are somehow connected, related to, or made to be a part of real life. Much of his writing still influences the work of educators and policymakers today (Beinecke 1998).

When we read into the literature on Kilpatrick, it is often stated that he was "a student of Dewey's." According to some writers, he was a student of Dewey's in that he heard various lectures by Dewey, not that he actually studied under Dewey in some systematic regard. Kilpatrick began work on his doctorate at Teachers College in 1909, completing it in 1915, and going on to a long and quite distinguished career at Columbia University. He was always regarded as a "disciple of Dewey" although Dewey never acknowledged such. Additionally, his work and writing surrounding the use of projects in teaching is something that Dewey never particularly espoused, nor is there any record of Dewey endorsing his work.

Like Dewey, Kilpatrick wrote prolifically over his working lifetime in academia but is mostly remembered for his 1918 article on the Project Method, a relatively small and obscure piece of work. Most people forget that Kilpatrick was a historian first and an educational theorist second, or that he made several quite significant contributions in educational history (Chipman and McDonald 1980).

While Dewey believed that the schools were the tool of social reform, Kilpatrick's primary belief was that the teaching of all subjects and subject matter should become real and related to the lives of the students. Chipman and McDonald (1980) state,

> As a fledgling graduate student, Kilpatrick had some serious reservations about Monroe's teaching methods. Basically, Kilpatrick believed Monroe failed to indicate how history lessons were relevant to contemporary times. "In fact," stated Kilpatrick, "If you questioned the people who studied under Monroe they couldn't have told you just what they were getting, except that they were learning who did this a thousand years ago, and when he did it and things like that, mostly dates. . . . During his first year as a history teacher, Kilpatrick taught both at Teachers College and Pratt Institute. For the most part, Kilpatrick followed the standard textbook approach of teaching. During the summers when local teachers arrived to update their credentials, he began experimenting with his presentations. In these sessions, he tried not to be too concerned with dates or names; instead he tried to present the subject in such a style that the students would relate these historical lessons to contemporary events. In so doing, he constantly fluctuated his emphasis on past events with current situations. His object was to allow his student a chance to problem-solve current events by using relevant facts from the past. (71–72)

Ellsworth Collings

Another progressive writer and theorist whose name is frequently associated with the project method, learning by doing, and similar methods is Ellsworth Collings. Under the direction of William Heard Kilpatrick, Collings earned his doctorate from Teachers College around 1920. He held several administrative positions in various schools before securing a professorship at the University of Oklahoma in 1922 (Garrett 2000).

Collings enjoyed a long and respected career at the University of Oklahoma writing prolifically about project teaching. He is noted and best remembered for his dissertation turned book—*An Experiment with a Project Curriculum*—published in 1926. In his writings, he described some elaborate and extensive efforts involving project teaching that were considered admirable at the time because of their extreme nature.

Unfortunately, in recent years, the truth and credibility of the work has been called to question as historians have attempted to piece together the claims made in his writings, particularly the claims concerning a typhoid outbreak in a small community (Knoll 1996). Regardless, it is still believed that his work has been quite influential in the design of policy and programs over the years.

Harold Rugg

Many educators and theorists trace the origins of the integrated curriculum to the work, writing, and philosophies of Harold Rugg. His name is forever attached to what has come to be called the "Social Reconstructionist Movement" (Stern and Riley 2001; Pahl 2001).

To make a very complicated story very simple, the social reconstructionist movement was an effort by scholars of the social sciences to use public education as the means to solve many problems inherent in a pluralistic society. The movement came about as the country was rebuilding after World War I and just before the economic crisis of the Great Depression. To summarize the thinking of Rugg and other social reconstructionists, Stern and Riley (2001) state,

> Rugg and the Social Reconstructionists viewed the role of the teacher as that of a facilitator who guided students to use the tools of critical thinking and problem solving to study real-world problems in the hope of preserving and building a more equitable democratic society in the United States. As Progressives, they never doubted that the tools of the scientific method coupled with the American spirit were capable of solving these problems (H. O. Rugg, 1939). They were convinced, however, that economic and social gaps between the rich and the poor were stifling American democracy, closing

down avenues of opportunity, and blocking creativity. Rugg believed those issues needed to be studied through the school curriculum so that all Americans would "see the light," first to address and then to rectify those problems. For Rugg, that was the beauty of democracy—citizens could express their freedom and exercise their liberty by studying, voting, and changing the system. (56)

A person's background and experiences will always influence any professional practice. Likewise, a person's academic specialty most certainly brings a perspective to his or her teaching. As a university professor of educational leadership, I must often stop, rethink, and not allow my musician/arts-educator background to impede progress or the general good. The beauty of democracy and democratic processes is that even the ignorant and narrow-minded rightfully have their say. When Rugg was teaching during the Great Depression era, he wrote and encouraged students to look beyond the obvious and ask difficult social questions. As the writings of Rugg reached more and more people, he came under serious and unfair media attack for upsetting the status quo. Nash (1995) states,

My examination of Rugg's books leads me to conclude that most of those who attacked them seem not to have read them (a situation duplicated in the History Standards controversy of 1994–95). Rugg's own analysis of the controversy begins with a chapter entitled "I Haven't Read the Books, But ___!" He explains that as he criss-crossed the country by train to defend his books: "Over and over again it came. 'I haven't read the books, but,' in essence, 'they are bad' from young and old, man and woman alike." Charged with Marxist or Communist leanings, Rugg found himself defending his textbook discussion of whether all Americans shared in the rising standard of living that had resulted from the development of industrial capitalism, Rugg entirely omitted discussion of the chronic industrial warfare that punctuated the 1870's through the 1920's, confining himself to a discussion of how the rapid increase in worker wages from 1850–1900 trailed off and how national income, by the late 1920's, was very unevenly distributed. But this was enough to touch off a wave of censorship on the grounds that young Americans who studied from Rugg's books would think poorly of their country and would be incited to class conflict. (49)

PROMINENT INSTITUTIONS

The emergence of progressive ideas in the schools did not come about quickly. In fact, there are many social science scholars who argue that such ideals have never taken any particularly serious form in the schools, but have only been "dabbled with." But at any rate, as progressive ideologies emerged and began to be seen in the schools, the names of some particular institutions of higher education seem forever attached. Likewise, as we read the historical literature, we run across names of school systems that seemed prominent for period(s) of time and then faded. An in-depth analysis of their contributions is clearly beyond the scope of this book. Instead, this section is intended to share an overview of prominent names and various tendencies we have seen over the years.

The University of Chicago

Clearly, the institutional name that is seen the most frequently is the University of Chicago. This was the academic home of Dewey's earliest work. The University of Chicago is a very select, private university situated in a part of Chicago's most elite area. Founded in 1890 primarily with funding from the Rockefeller family and land given by department-store giant Marshall Field, the new university was situated in the upscale Hyde Park suburb of Chicago. From the beginning, the University of Chicago was a "break the mold" institution with comparatively liberal ideas and curricular offerings. Additionally, the university would admit women and minorities when other universities did not. So it would seem logical that a person like Dewey, who believed adamantly in social development and change, would be attracted to such an institution.

But of sorts, it is an ongoing irony that Dewey's early work began at the University of Chicago. The original mission of the university was clearly intended to appeal to the elite and the liberal. There is a great deal of professional literature to assert and support that these social ideals are not those typically shared by persons who would be attracted to the teaching profession then or today. We know from a great deal of quality research that those individuals who are attracted to the profession of teaching tend to come from more modest socioeconomic backgrounds and tend to express more conservative ideals. One need only visit the university to realize that Dewey's ideas were a focus, but hardly made manifest there. During the preparation of this manuscript, I visited the campus of the university. While I was unable to visit classrooms and such, I was able to tour the library. For persons whose educational background includes having studied at modest, state-supported, primarily teacher-training institutions, it is awe inspiring to see such grandeur in architecture, landscaping, and research facilities. This is not the typical experience of persons entering the field of teaching. Even those who were fortunate enough to study at large state-supported research institutions probably did not enjoy such lavish surroundings. It is clear from the outside looking in that students come to the University of Chicago having a different set of experiences, backgrounds, perspectives, and finances—all of which are not the typical profile of those seeking to enter the teaching field. It is also interesting that while this prestigious institution that has contributed so significantly to our profession closed its College of Education in 2001.

Teachers College

Teachers College of Columbia University (founded in 1887) is the other institution whose name appears frequently in the early literature surrounding the progressive movement. The mission of the college was primarily to upgrade the skills, knowledge, and awareness of the teachers who would teach the poor, migrant, and inner-city children of the New York schools. Just like the University of Chicago, this would appear to be the perfect academic home for those who believed in education as the means by which society would become more equitable. From the 1890s to about the late 1920s, there were a number of scholars who vacillated between the University of Chicago and Teachers College. For those who were able, these were the places of choice to study to become a teacher.

Bank Street College of Education

Another institution that has become almost synonymous with Dewey and child-centered teaching is the Bank Street College of Education. This professional graduate school originated in New York around 1916 as a project by some civic-minded women—among them Lucy Sprague Mitchell—who generally believed that teacher training of the time was grossly inadequate and generally discounted the needs of children. After securing external funding to do what would today likely be called "action research," Mitchell and her colleagues embarked on a series of ventures that evolved into the purchase of an old building on Bank Street. By 1930, the program's status had reached that of a legitimate mode of graduate study in progressive teacher preparation. The entire focus of the Bank Street plan was to make teaching and schooling a more humane effort and to generate problem-solving strategies as a way of life (Grinberg 2002). Grinberg (2002) states,

> The difference in the types of experiences that students at Bank Street talked about was laid in the ways in which they were taught, which invited them to think, to challenge, to make connections and to become passionate about teaching and learning. The passion was contagious; the faculty was also passionate in their own teaching. The passion was also manifested in the loving of the subjects taught. (1428)

Zilversmit (1993) has written quite extensively about public school systems whose early efforts boosted support of the often fought-over notion that progressive education could actually work in real schools with real children. We find numerous writings of the resounding success of schools in Illinois in such areas as Lake Forest, Winnetka, and Waukegan as they attempted—with noted success—to move beyond the traditional mode of education and make their local public schools a model to be admired. Other school systems whose efforts became a model for success included Gary, Indiana (Zilversmit 1984), Arthurdale, West Virginia (Perlstein 1996), and Dalton, Massachusetts need reference. As we examine and compare the success stories, we find some glaring similarities. We must remember that we are looking at aggregates, not anecdotes and—just as when interpreting research findings—that we are observing tendencies, not absolutes.

First, when we look at both early and contemporary success stories, we find that such school systems and success stories tended to fall in the developing industrial northeast, or on the west coast.

Second, such school systems and success stories tended to be found in communities that fell into two categories. Either the communities were being developed by reform-minded, middle-class, transformational-type civic leaders or in the communities that were notedly affluent and were strongly established. Then we did not—nor do we often today—find the ideals of progressive education successfully implemented in communities that were (or are) poor. We have known for years that teachers in the more affluent school systems have the time to deal with progressive education initiatives and concerns. The teachers in less affluent school systems typically must spend far more of their professional time dealing with social issues and problems that are not typically found in affluent areas.

Third, regardless of the socioeconomic status of the communities concerned, such initiatives and reforms never came about without a significant struggle from the leadership of the day. Selling such ideas to the public has always been problematic because we know the public has always been skeptical of such. Progressive ideals and initiatives have always frightened the conservative of society. We know that the more diverse the population, the harder the fight to bring about progressive ideals and initiatives and the harder the fight to keep such initiatives in place. It is often argued that the two social institutions that most influence society—the school and the church—are the most resistant to change. Consequently, a consistent reluctance to change, while understandable, is a nuisance to reform-minded leaders.

Fourth, successful progressive initiatives have always been seen when and where there was an adequate cash flow to support such initiative and experimentation. When cash flow patterns change, so do the efforts at progressive innovation. For years we have seen a pattern of lost funding coupled with a return to the traditional. It is certainly fair to say that the success of progressive innovations has always been directly related to the wealth of the community.

Fifth, successful progressive initiatives and innovations have never lived past the demographic structures that created them. When the demographic and socioeconomic structure changed (typically to include minorities and the less affluent), progressive ideals and initiatives tend to disappear. Likewise, although schools and school systems initiated progressive reforms after having embraced common ideologies, there were always differing results in every city and town (Plank, Scotch, and Gamble 1996).

Finally, just as the thesis of this book, the bottom-line question then was no different than any other educational question or squabble of today. No matter where or how progressive initiatives have been tried or how well they reportedly succeeded, there has never been a clear, understandable, consensus definition of or answer to the question of "what is progressive education?"

VISIBLE INFLUENCES ON PROGRESSIVE REFORM

Over the years, there were a number of books published and events of notoriety that unquestionably influenced many progressive initiatives. Perhaps the most conspicuous event in American history to wreak havoc on progressive ideals occurred in 1957 when the Russians launched Sputnik. The United States was quite embarrassed that another country, especially one whose political and social ideals differed so much from our own, beat us in the race to outer space. As is typical in the face of many national crises, the schools and teachers—and in this case in particular, progressive education—took the blame. It was reported that school curriculums were not focused on content, and that children were learning to like themselves and explore their feelings rather than use a common body of information to solve problems. It was argued then, just as today, that our schools do not produce enough persons trained in math and science. Although such arguments are always subject to valid criticism from those who understand the workings of the system, it nevertheless is still a perpetual battle. But, at any rate, the pressure was on to make math and science teaching more rigorous and meaningful in such a way as to produce thinkers and problem solvers. Bybee (1998) said,

> Curriculum reformers of the Sputnik era shared a common vision. Across disciplines and within the educational community, reformers generated enthusiasm for their initiatives. They would replace the current content of topics and information with a curriculum based on the conceptually fundamental ideas and the modes of scientific inquiry and mathematical problem solving. The reform would replace textbooks with instructional materials that included films, activities, and readings. No longer would schools' science and mathematics programs emphasize information, terms, and applied aspects of content. Rather, students would learn the structures and procedures of science and mathematics disciplines. (2)

DeBoer (1998) describes Sputnik era reform in this way:

> The Sputnik era was a distinctive period in the history of science education in the United States. It is often considered a time of conservative reform because of its emphasis on rigor and discipline as opposed to the more progressive child-centered approaches that both preceded and followed it. It is

reminiscent of the science education reforms of the 1890's that were led by Harvard President and chemist, Charles Eliot, and which culminated in the report of the Committee of Ten. It also bears similarity to the spirit of reform of the early 1980's, particularly the report of the national Commission on Excellence in Education, *A Nation at Risk*. Although we can easily point to lessons that were learned during the Sputnik era, it is difficult to say how long those lessons will be remembered. Attitudes in science education seem to oscillate over time between those that favor the mastery of content as it is understood and organized by the adult mind and those that favor adapting the content of the curriculum to the particular interests of individual students. Without a clearer and more fundamental sense of what we are trying to accomplish, there is little reason to think that a movement between these two distinctive ideologies will not continue in the future.

It is interesting that two quite significant yet diametrically opposed pieces of research surfaced over a period of about thirty years that have created controversy but little support of reform. In 1930 an effort began by the Progressive Education Association, headed by Ralph Tyler, came to be known as the Eight-Year Study. The work of this project, while hardly conclusive, still has policy implications today. The study involved about 300 colleges and universities who were willing to bypass traditional admission requirements and admit students who had studied in nontraditional (progressive) high schools. It was clearly the intent of the study to support the effectiveness of progressive ideals and many writers think it does not do so particularly well (Kahne 1995). Of the findings of the Eight-Year Study, Schugurensky and Aguirre (2002b) say,

> Although none of the students who participated in the Eight-Year Study went on to make a profound impact on the colleges or universities they attended, and although the findings of the Eight-Year Study were hardly revolutionary, some of them were indeed significant. First and foremost, the Eight-Year Study determined that college success is not predetermined by the high-school curriculum requirements. Secondly, students at more experimental schools tended to perform more highly than less experimental schools—despite such hardships as economic poverty. Also, the Eight-Year Study found that integrative approaches to the curriculum—rather than breaking it down into disciplines—produced highly favorable results. In the end, however, the Eight-Year Study fell into the shadow of World War II, and its outcomes and impact were minimal. (1)

At the opposite extreme of the Eight-Year Study, Project Follow Through began in 1967 and ended in 1995. The effort was begun as a part of President Johnson's War on Poverty that resulted in many federal dollars flowing into the public schools. Prior to that time, such had not been the case. Project Follow Through is often cited as the largest educational study ever attempted and, in short, the findings of the study strongly support the notion that teacher-directed instructional methods are more effective for disadvantaged children. The prominence and success of the Direct Instruction Model comes forth most prominently in the Follow Through reports, but Direct Instruction (DI) proponents will generally assert that the DI model is not for everyone (Grossen 1995). Of the fate of Project Follow Through, Watkins (1995) says,

> Project Follow Through, the largest experiment ever undertaken to find effective methods for teaching disadvantaged children, discovered such a teaching method at a cost of nearly a billion dollars. They call it "Direct Instruction," a highly structured, teacher-led teaching method. . . . Between 1968–1976, achievement data from 51 school districts, using nine different teaching approaches (models), ranging from Direct Instruction to Child-Centered and Open Education, were collected from nearly 10,000 children each year until they completed grade three. . . . Direct Instruction (DI) outperformed both traditionally taught comparison groups and all other tested models. DI outstripped them not only in Basic Skills (word knowledge, spelling, language, and math computation), and in Cognitive-Conceptual Skills (reading comprehension, math concepts and problem solving), but in Self-Concept as well—the category emphasized by the "progressive" teaching models. . . . Essentially, the Follow Through findings were buried in a sea of disinformation. School districts never found out which models worked, and JDRP (the Federal Joint Dissemination Review Panel) defeated the very purpose of its own existence. (1)

TOWARD A LITERATE POPULATION

The word *literate* takes on various meanings but for our discussion here, let us simply assert that literate means the possession of a level of formal education and skill whereby a person can read, write, and effectively communicate with the remainder of society and is not dependent upon others for information. Prior to the emergence of the Progressive Era, American society had done little, or been unable, to support or encourage what can be considered a generally literate population. It had traditionally been the children who were of extreme privilege or lived in communities that collectively had the resources to offer some organized educational experiences at the elementary level who became the literate of society. The extremely privileged were able to go to neighboring towns and attend some sort of secondary institution when they were of appropriate age. In the more remote areas where people were particularly poor or were some distance from the school, children often did not attend school because it simply was not possible. It is fair to say that during those years there was a very distinct line between the segment of the population who was literate and that which was not. It is an interesting truth that the educational challenges of 100 years ago very much parallel those of today. At that time, just as today, it was far more often the poor of society who were ill educated than the affluent.

Dewey was determined to see his ideas put into practice and within two years after creating the Department of Pedagogy at the University of Chicago he embarked on one aspect of his work that continues to influence many progressive thinkers of today—he and his wife founded the Dewey Laboratory School at the University of Chicago. Initially, the school was quite small but grew considerably in the seven years that it operated under his direction. According to many writers and historians, although there is still a great deal of interest in the school (what went on, the success of the endeavors, and similar evaluations), the records that were kept were somewhat lacking (Chall 2000). The only particularly beneficial documents that have survived are such things as board meeting minutes and personal commentaries from teachers. Such documents as lesson plans or teaching materials that might assist in studying the effectiveness of the school and its programs have been lost, but some other teacher-written documents are still in existence (Tanner 1997).

According to Tanner (1997), Dewey and the Lab School faculty experienced many of the same frustrations then as teachers express concern over today—particularly the professional autonomy/intellectual freedom that is taken for granted by university-level teachers, but conspicuously absent in the role of the elementary school teacher. Tanner (1997) states,

From Dewey came one of the first pronouncements that elementary teachers should have intellectual freedom. Today, however, we speak of professional autonomy rather than intellectual freedom. According to Shepard (1995), for example, university researchers who want to help teachers find new ways to assess student learning should take care not to "undermine professional autonomy" (p. 38). Her concern is understandable. A wave of legislation on accountability in the 1970's and 1980's reflected the view that teachers are technicians, not professionals. Policy makers embraced what Darling-Hammond and Snyder (1992) call "the bureaucratic model" (p. 17). . . . Discussions in the 1990's began to focus on teacher empowerment and autonomy. In fact, it was almost impossible to read an article on teaching without coming across some mention of professional autonomy. After decades of neglect, it would seem that the professional model, as Dewey conceived it, is making a comeback. Or is it? (67)

This will be discussed further in chapter 4, but for now let us understand that as Dewey began his work, society was ready for some significant change in the business and operations of schools. It must be remembered that due to circumstances and norms, the status of teaching and teacher training at the time was such that it would hardly be recognized today. For example, it was really not until the 1920s that it came to be expected anywhere that teachers would actually earn a college degree. Even as late as the 1960s, it was not terribly uncommon to see persons teaching in the public schools with less than a four-year university degree.

But the progressive movement was not immune to the same fate as many other "movements" that have come about in more recent years. When multiple theorists and philosophers adhere to an idea, the opportunity for multiple interpretations and implementations tends to come about. The progressive education movement was no exception. From the beginning, many adamantly decried the very ideals that education can be a democratic process to further support the ideals of a democratic society. Others accepted the ideals, but used them to support personal or professional agendas that were not necessarily in keeping with Dewey's original intent. Cohen (1998) states,

The problems that Dewey worried most about did not arise in schools and reached far beyond education. One was the growth of industrialism, increasing economic inequality, and the political inequality that resulted from concentrations of wealth and poverty. Another was the collapse of organic communities as social bonds and torn by capitalist economic relations, mass migrations of agricultural workers to cities, and new patterns of factory work. Still another was the greater importance of knowledge to economic

and social life owing to scientific and technical progress by the rapidly diminishing knowledge required from individual workers owing to increased
specialization. These were the same problems that had preoccupied Karl
Marx and many other nineteenth-century thinkers. Dewey did not discover
them, for they were the intellectual chatter—and fear—of the century, discovered and rediscovered more times than anyone could count. His diagno-
sis of modern social ills was in no sense original. (428)

CHANGING SCHOOLS TO MEET THE PEOPLE

The business of teaching and learning contains inherent difficulties that
are peculiar to this business alone. But where difficulties arise in this business (difficulties that probably happen less often in other service professions than in education) is the overwhelming urge to make the people fit
the school or what we perceive the school should be. The emergence of
the progressive ideals caused the leaders of the day to rethink many conventionally held ideas about what the schools should do, and as such
caused many changes to come about in what actually went on inside
schools. By doing so, the schools could accommodate more children with
larger variations in background and experience. But in order to accommodate this movement toward what is called "inclusion" today, programs
and services had to be designed, created, and implemented.

Then, as now, the schools are charged with a monumental task in which
we are accountable to all yet supported by few, expected to produce with
meager resources, and positioned to never please anyone. The Progressive
Education Association was formed in 1919 (Schugurensky and Aguirre
2002a) but even as late as the 1930s with the progressive movement in full
swing, there was not a particularly clear direction recognized and acknowledged by all (Redefer 1948). Although the organization disbanded
in 1955 (Ogden 1992), at that time, just as now, there were many educators who call themselves progressive but did not particularly espouse the
ideas of Dewey. Redefer (1948) says,

Progressive education was born in revolt against the prevailing mass educational methods and against a public-school system that reflected many of
the values permeating American society. Francis W. Parker was one of those
who rebelled against the routine nature of schooling: it was he who coined

the expression "the child-centered school." His effort to focus attention on the individual child was in harmony with the values of the society which stressed individual competition and individual success; it was nurtured by a slowly growing concern for the welfare of children which, in turn, was strengthened by the advent of the science of psychology. (49)

But as the movement gained momentum, some similar attributes and characteristics were seen frequently. Schugurensky and Aguirre (2002a) state,

> Two of the main principles fostered in the Progressive Movement were continuity and interaction. Continuity is the principle that each learning experience be nurtured by the previous experience. Therefore, from a Progressive standpoint, the learning process is gradual. The organizational thought process that relates all experiential processes is something Dewey named the "Logical Organization of the Subject Matter." The second principle, interaction, denotes the concept that what was learned may possibly need revisions, adaptations, or be discarded all together because further research has claimed it to be false. Essentially, from this standpoint, assumptions need to be challenged in the continual search for absolute truth. Thus, the interaction principle encouraged experimentalism, verification, and reconstruction. (2)

The progressive movement is credited with the introduction of various programs and services not previously seen in the schools. Such programs and services included vocational guidance counseling, psychological counseling, and school lunches. It was during this time that we began to see school health programs and the services of social workers in the schools. The introduction of such services and programs forever changed the focus and certainly broadened the scope of schools in general. By doing so, the schools were able to serve more of the population, and schooling in general would become more attractive to the population at large. Sedlak and Scholssman (1985) state,

> The principal concern of the "progressives" were the first- and second-generation immigrant, working-class children who entered the schools in unprecedented numbers during the early twentieth century. The overriding rationale for virtually all "progressive" innovations was to attract such children to school and hold them as long as possible. "Progressives" introduced free school lunches, for example, to achieve this goal. Hungry or

malnourished children made poor scholars, were susceptible to disease, and consequently were likely to be absent from school, the "progressives" claimed. "The brain cannot gnaw on problems while the stomach is gnawing on its empty self" observed one proponent. By World War I, public schools in approximately one hundred cities were serving meals to needy children. (373)

It is argued by many that the expansion of school-based services, while well intended in purpose, reached far beyond the bounds of feasibility and practicality while others argue that the reforms were not sufficient (Tyack 1975). It was during this time (circa 1940s) that the public began to see the work of the schools cross over into the court system for children who had been so unfortunate as to find themselves in trouble with the law. It was then that we began to see workers from the schools going into homes to intervene in matters of family life, personal health, or hygiene. Then, as now, the question of boundaries is a messy one when the basis of the question is the best interest and safety of children. For example, if we bring the question forward about fifty years, most of these educators could never have imagined that the schools of the 1990s would be called upon to distribute condoms (and explain their use) to lessen the likelihood of children becoming infected with fatal sexually transmitted diseases. The inexact nature of the work of schools will always create nebulous professional boundaries. But when asking the question of whether progressives attained their goals, Sedlak and Scholssman (1985) state,

> The "progressive" vision of the school as an all-purpose social service institution did not come close to being implemented. Several of the proposed innovations were largely abortive, while those that were institutionalized either had much narrower ends and means than the "progressives" envisioned or survived only because external funding subsidized the venture. Any notion that local public schools have willingly embraced a wide variety of nonacademic social service and curricular innovations seems unwarranted. (381)

It is ironic and almost comical that the same arguments have been tossed back and forth for over 100 years but with no clear indicator of who has won this ideological battle. Then, just as today, the early reformers all had the same honest intentions, but varieties in interpretations. Most educators and scholars today doubt the battle will ever be won.

Chapter Three

Progressive Education in Action: What Really Happens

Teaching in an inquiry mode requires taking risks; risks that students will not learn, risks that the psychic reward of teaching that are so important will not be present, risks that the teacher's authority as the arbiter of knowledge will somehow be called into question. Such risks make it safer for teachers to teach in their tried and true traditional methods.

—E. Wood, 1990

It is no secret that the business of teaching and learning is far more complex than most people realize. As such, in an effort to stay afloat in a system that must continue to produce, many very complex ideas become "watered down" or at least become so oversimplified that they mislead the unknowing. Such oversimplifications may come about in such questions as "What does progressive education look like?" It is practically impossible to visit a public or private school anywhere in this country and not see elements, ideas, and attributes of progressive education ideas in classrooms, instructional practices, and the general manner in which schools are organized and managed. As a teacher, trainer of teachers, and university professor, I have never ceased to be amazed at the frequency and intensity at which progressive ideas dominate. Someone who does the work that I do can scarcely imagine a school administrator visiting a classroom and suggesting that a teacher utilize instructional or management practices that even remotely resemble anything other than or outside of that which can be considered progressive—even if that perception is flawed.

If we were to visit a school, look around, and talk to certain people, some striking similarities would become evident regardless of the location, level of school, or the population being served. We would likely hear some common verbiage, most of which comes about in relation to some of the most commonly held beliefs about what progressive education is and is not. For example, it is common to hear school administrators, under pressure to produce the outcomes demanded of the current political climate, to say to a visitor, "We teach strictly hands-on" or "Our teachers stress higher-level thinking over the mere acquisition of facts." It can hardly be argued that such ideas are not noble and unquestionably an effort to be admired by any. But, unfortunately, the political rhetoric and misunderstood educational verbiage surrounding those ideas often falls short of the real outcomes (Wichmann 1980).

In this chapter, let us look at some quite prominent and popular progressive ideas for which a diligent effort has been made to translate into physical practice. Despite the most honest of intentions, we will see that many, if not most, of these ideas somehow manage to lose their focus in the translation. This should not be interpreted to mean that such ideas are inherently bad. Actually, most would assume and accept that quality teaching at any level includes such practices. The problematic element here is the notion of extremism—taking an idea beyond where it was intended to fall.

PROGRESSIVE TERMINOLOGIES

Good Intentions

There has been much written in recent years exposing the polarities between traditional education and progressive education ideologies, much of which is extreme and unfair, creating adversarial relationships between the two schools of thought as though there must be a winner in a war. Other writings, however, have attempted to create a fair balance between the two ideas and the reader should assume this to be my intent. It is interesting to note in the research and anecdotal observation that schools that are considered successful by today's standards usually demonstrate a balance between the two extremes both in philosophy and practice. According to Hirsch (1996), far too many writers and critics unfairly focus on the negative aspects of the other extreme and do not allow an educated reader to make an informed decision. The crux of the problem here is that

patron's name:Woldemariam, Michael

title:Personal epistemology in
author:Bendixen, Lisa D.
item id:31786102618706
due:8/24/2010,23:59

title:The power of pedagogy
author:Leach, Jenny.
item id:31786101378773
due:8/24/2010,23:59

title:Dilemmas of culture in Af
author:Coe, Cati.
item id:31786102063275
due:8/24/2010,23:59

title:the promise and failure o
author:Norris, Norman Dale, 1958
item id:31786101823103
due:8/24/2010,23:59

while many of the ideas might make sense on the surface, when the actual practices are examined more closely, they are found to be seriously flawed and not in keeping with the theories of progressive education. This is essentially creating the same parental dilemma of wanting to respect the child's privacy but needing to know if the child is hiding something illicit in the bedroom. It is a critical and indisputable fact that as badly as progressive education ideals have been applied, it must be remembered that all those ideas surfaced in an attempt to help, not hinder.

Mere Facts versus Higher Thinking

Perhaps the most frequently cited extreme in ideology is the mode of teaching referred to as the "mere acquisition of facts" as opposed to "higher-level thinking." This idea is usually backed with further verbiage asserting the desire to create "lifelong learners" or citizens who are "independently capable of learning anything on their own." The idea between the two extremes is that the mode of teaching whereby children are taught a body of simple factual information for later use is of far less benefit than the teaching of skills that supposedly train the learner to think critically or to explore so they might eventually discover those facts for themselves. The idea is that through the teaching of such higher-order thinking skills, the student has no need to retain a body of factual information because having attained the necessary higher skills, the requisite body of information will either come about automatically or can be located when needed. This idea is often further supported with such statements as "in this age of information, facts are soon outdated, so let's not waste instructional time on them"—which sounds plausible to forward-thinking people and seems to fit nicely with the thinking of John Dewey, but is seriously flawed for several reasons. Does factual data actually change? Most thinkers would say no.

First, a fact, by definition, is a piece of information that is known, generally known to be, or generally accepted as true based upon the current knowledge base. Facts are useful pieces of information as opposed to trivia, which is true information, usually of an anecdotal nature, but is generally of no use outside the particular interest of the individual. As people learn more, what was once accepted as fact may be supplemented by newer and better information, but the basis on which the new information came about will not simply "go away." For example, it was once believed—by well-intentioned and the most well-educated individuals of the time—that to bleed someone was an appropriate and effective way of removing an infectious medium from the body. Today, medical professionals know that bleeding a person is not a particularly healthy thing to do. Likewise, it was only within the last thirty to thirty-five years that medical professionals truly believed that electroshock therapy was useful and effective in the treatment of some emotional disorders. The fact that bleeding or electroshock treatments are now known to be quite undesired manners of treating certain ailments (at least to such an extent as they were previously used) does not mean that physicians do not need to know that such practices ever existed. It is by knowing of these practices that we know we should no longer rely on such practices. Therefore, it is a false notion that a fact can simply become "outdated" and have no more use. The fact that Columbus discovered America in 1492 or that the Civil War ended in 1865 is not trivia. What ensued following Columbus's discovery is not trivia. The facts surrounding the onset of the Civil War are not trivia. This is all factual information that well-educated people need to know and it will not become "outdated." Unfortunately, I have on various occasions been the victim of such archaic thinking; a particularly ill-informed school administrator stood before the faculty and stated the very quote in the previous paragraph regarding "outdated" facts.

The educational thinkers and leaders who speak adamantly of the "antifactual" mode of teaching are unquestionably well intentioned but seem to miss the most basic tenet of human communication. In order for any society (or section thereof) to communicate, there must first exist a common body of information—simple factual data that all must know and hold before communication (defined as the exchange of information) can occur. It is simply wrong to assume that acquiring factual data in a person's memory does not in any manner constitute quality learning. In any society, one will be expected to abide by certain laws governing one's daily conduct and social behavior as well as familial and financial matters. For example, there are entirely separate sets of laws governing the owning and operating of a motor vehicle that, for the safety of the individual and everyone else on the road, one must know from memory. In short, one must know traffic laws so well that their practice is not a matter of conscious thought, but instead is automatic. In any civilized society, there are sets of behavioral expectations that may not be written down as laws but are certainly expected as etiquette or "common manners." Clearly it would be absurd to think that one would not need to have these laws or manners, essentially bits of factual data, committed to memory in exchange for the skills necessary to "figure out the laws" when the need should arise.

Such thinking also actually contradicts one of the most basic tenets of our American legal system, which is that ignorance of the law is not an excuse for having broken the law. The "antifact" type of educators often cite that "an attorney doesn't know every aspect of the law but knows where to find that information should he or she need it." On the surface, this appears to be true but again is seriously misleading. Certainly we want attorneys who know how to analyze particular situations and solve legal problems. But can one imagine an attorney not holding a body of legal information in his or her memory that included such things as court procedures, divisions of law practice, or the most basic of civil rights? Shanker (1996) illustrates the point,

> One challenge to sound education for democracy programs is posed by the contention that what matters in teaching democratic citizenship is the teaching of "critical thinking" skills, and little else. Closely related to this is the attitude that considers all curricular content to be equal, and champions the proposition that all that is required of students to be good citizens is that they "learn how to learn." Proponents of this position often argue that the pace of knowledge is expanding so rapidly, it quickly becomes "obsolete," and by extension, not worth learning. . . . Unfortunately the proponents of teaching skills and little else offer a false dichotomy between "content" and "process." I do not wish to fall into that trap, so let me be clear: both are important. Of course, developing thinking skills is a major goal of education in democracy. How else can one make a wise choice between alternatives—whether it be taking a position on a political issue, deciding for whom to vote in an election, or avoiding the manipulative techniques used by some political figures—if one is equipped with and had practice in this area? (1–2)

To further illustrate the point, as a pianist, I certainly do not know every piece of piano music ever written. However, I hold to memory a collective body of factual and conceptual information—namely, a relationship between lines and spaces, melodic notation, rhythmic notation, and stylistically appropriate performance practices. Because I hold such a collective body of data to memory, I am able to learn, master, and perform any unfamiliar piece of piano literature I should so desire. Lacking this requisite body of "factual" information, I would never be able to independently learn a new piece of music. Instead, I would be dependent upon someone else to teach me the music by rote, or in the alternative, to mimic what I may have heard with no conceptual understanding of what I am performing. Bernardo (1997) asserts that the extremes between "what to think" and "how to think" are mythical, or at least created problems. He states,

> There is no battle between learning and learning how to learn. The whole progressive movement has for many years been moving away from the content (the what) and toward process (the how). The attempt to teach children how to think has been a dismal failure when we consider the terrible record of student achievement. All the important research about how kids learn points to the need for specific content as the foundation for any kind of learning. There is no such thing as an all-purpose thinking skill. Every field requires its specific kind of skills. Moreover, the dichotomy between content and skills is patently false. You can't think without facts and information. The more one's mind is well stocked with information, the better is one's thinking process. What is really needed to develop thinking skills is what Hirsch calls "a generous number of carefully chosen exemplary facts." The notion spouted by progressives that children learn better by moving from concepts to facts rather than vice versa is utter nonsense, and yet we find it even in much of the legislation supporting the reforms. (5)

But the battle over factual data and its commitment to memory does go deeper. Factual data is not limited to tiny pieces of information but also includes "processes," which are the collective use of tiny pieces of information and tenets or phenomena that cannot be conceptualized when lacking the support of the common body of information. Unfortunately, the higher-order thinking question is taken much too far, extending beyond the bounds of good sense and reality. Jesness (2000) makes the following analogy:

> To learn the Periodic Table of the Elements is mere rote, but to square dance while imagining oneself to be an electron orbiting around a nucleus—that is

higher-level thinking. A child who is able to recite the Gettysburg Address is exhibiting mere knowledge, the bottom of Bloom's Taxonomy, but one who wrote "teecher stincks" was exhibiting judgment, Bloom's pinnacle. (2)

As scholars and practitioners, we must find some balance between the two extremes in ideas. Consequently, learning how to learn must somehow include the mastery of a body of factual data in many disciplines.

Cookie-Cutter Education

In the traditional–progressive war, one of the most common terminologies to come forth refers to a "cookie-cutter" style of curriculum design and implementation. The idea here is that since no two people are identical, then the processes by which two people are educated can never be identical. In a wholly theoretical context, this idea seems plausible but is flawed for one simple reason: it can hardly be interpreted to mean that education is a totally individualized service providing something for everyone with no duplications anywhere—and it is certainly true that Dewey's philosophy rejected this idea. This verbiage creates a false mental image of a practice that really doesn't exist. Although learning may be an inherently personal endeavor, public education is an endeavor that must consider the masses. From a standpoint of pure practicality, our system cannot design several billion systems of education so that no two people are educated exactly alike. Here again, it is all too unfortunate that many ill-informed educational leaders discuss these ideas and toss about the verbiage of progressive education when they truly do not understand the depth of the concept.

Real Life and Relevance

In recognizing the ideas of Dewey, it is an important tenet of progressive education that what is taught and learned is intended to be useful so that students become productive citizens. To this end, we frequently hear the assumed progressive verbiage of "relevant." Unfortunately, such a word has various meanings to various people. The problems occur when the definition of relevant—which should be "eventually useful"—becomes a less realistic meaning, such as "immediate and dramatically different." We know that our schools are under constant pressure to produce results that are immediately visible, and appear to make drastic improvements that are easily seen. Matczynski, Rogus, Lasley, and Joseph (2000) state, "Regrettably, many teachers focus so exclusively on cultural relevance that they fail to see that students do not understand essential content. Urban schools must embrace both traditional and progressivist ideas, emphasizing the former in the elementary grades and the latter as students establish a solid knowledge base" (354).

But at the same time, the question of relevance must address not only usefulness and benefit but also practicality. Goodman (1969) argues that the years spent in school are often unrelated to the student's success at a profession or adulthood in general. He states,

> The belief that a highly industrialized society requires twelve to twenty years of prior processing of the young is an illusion or a hoax. The evidence is strong that there is no correlation between school performance and life achievement in any of the professions, whether medicine, law, engineering, journalism, or business. Moreover, research shows that for more modest clerical, technological, or semiskilled factory jobs there is no advantage in years of schooling or the possession of diplomas. We were not exactly savages in 1900 when only 6 per cent of adolescents graduated from high school. (98)

Somehow, the well-intended rhetoric becomes so idealized that we lose sight of the fact that not everything taught to or learned by children can be fun or instantaneously enlightening. There is an incorrect mind-set—probably an offshoot of some serious misapplication of Madelyn Hunter's ideas in the late 1970s—that each time a lesson is delivered children are presumed to know nothing at the beginning and hold mastery of a usable skill at the end. It is likewise erroneously assumed that the children had fun, were never troubled by any intellectual growing pains, and clearly understood how and why they would use this newly acquired information both immediately and forever. Obviously such an idea is utter nonsense, but it does exist and finds itself played out every day in schools across the country. Hirsch (2002) states,

> A lot of learning is, of necessity, pretty meaningless. The connection between the sound and the sense of many words is entirely arbitrary. That the words "brother" and "sister" sound like they do is, for a child, just a brute fact that has to be learned. But, once the arbitrary sound-sense connection

is learned, the meaningfulness of those words ensures that they will be re-membered. Meaningfulness implies connectedness by experiential associa-tion (episodic memory), by schematic structure (semantic memory), or by emotional associations. In the expert-novice experiments, it is thought that prior knowledge enables the expert not only to connect the elements of an experience, but also to pick out what is meaningful and salient in it. More-over, prior knowledge enables the expert to deduce more from the experi-ence than the novice can. A novice looking at the outside of an Italian villa wouldn't understand that it has an unseen central courtyard; the expert, equipped with prior knowledge, would comprehend the unseen interior courtyard as well as the exterior walls. (9)

Fragmented Subject Matter

We often hear in the verbiage of progressive education that traditional ed-ucational approaches tend to "fragment" subject matter into tiny pieces, thereby making what is learned less meaningful. Previously we discussed the difference between factual data and trivia. It is fair to say that while factual data is not an inherently bad thing, trivia is not without its place in the development of the educated mind. The problems occur when we have well-meaning educational leaders who attempt to force-fit an idea or link concepts when no such link really exists. As an example, some time ago, state-mandated high-stakes testing was forcing educators to do a number of things that most would not consider in the best interest of children. In an effort to create additional instruction that would supposedly influence test scores, I had a well-intended but clearly ill-informed curriculum spe-cialist say to me, "Music is very mathematical, so you can always link the two." The meaning here was that because there are attributes about music that are quite mathematical in nature (counting beats, subdividing beats, intervals between pitches, etc.), exposure to these musical elements would automatically strengthen the children's concepts of fractions. It would be hideously naïve to believe that working with rhythmic notation would be an appropriate substitute for the systematic study of fractions or the ap-propriate practice in their use.

The use of the verbiage of "fragmented" leads to a false mental image of children being taught isolated curricular components that have no rela-tion to one another, are not based in real life, and not appealing to the in-tellect of children. While it is difficult to envision any subject matter that stands entirely on its own with no influence or crossing over between disciplines, there most certainly is subject matter that can and possibly should be taught on its own merit without concern for how it crosses between disciplines. Such thinking is a clear demonstration of the belief that most educational reform is a matter rejecting the opposing position or ideology. Knowledgeable educational leaders must not fall victim to such behavior.

Hands-on, Project Teaching

There will forever be much discussion, argument, and disagreement between both sides of the traditional–progressive argument over the idea of hands-on, project-type teaching. It is unfortunate that we often hear ill-informed educational leaders equate "Dewey" and "progressive" with "projects" when we know from many decades of writing that it was William Heard Kilpatrick who was the proponent of projects. There is a false mind-set that instruction delivered via projects is inherently superior to any other. It is generally assumed that students completing projects are learning more, learning at higher levels, and are having fun in the process. This is a dangerous and naïve mind-set for many reasons and Dewey is often unfairly credited with this idea (McAninch 2000).

In a spirit of intellectual honesty, one can never assert that project teaching is an inherently bad idea. Project teaching, however, must always be called into question when the completion of the project entails far more time, resources, or personal energy—while producing no better outcomes—than more traditional modes of teaching (Sewall 2000). Of particular concern is when the benefit of the project is far less than if the instruction had been delivered in a more traditional and conservative manner.

TECHNOLOGY

There is much argument among educational leaders and thinkers as to the role that current technology is supposed to play in the education of children. While anything mechanical or electronic that is used in instruction is considered by some to be technology, the term seems to somehow limit itself to computers. In the progressive mind-set, everything about education is supposed to prepare children for the real world. Since computers are as much a part of our environment as a filing cabinet, telephone, or kitchen sink, it certainly makes sense that ensuring a child is comfortable with the use of computers is necessary, just as they should be able to use a telephone. In the mid-1960s, most American homes had phones, but there were many that did not. I remember as an elementary school-age child seeing representatives from the phone company bringing the most elaborate technological teaching devices of the day into the schools to teach children how to properly use the phone, telephone manners, and how to phone for police, medical, or fire assistance. By today's standards, this would seem silly, but it was necessary at the time.

But some false dichotomies seem to appear when educational leaders take the technology question to an extreme. There is a mind-set that because instruction is in some way, good or bad, linked to computer technology (or is based in technology) that instruction, learning, and retention are somehow improved. There is likewise a mind-set that because children are using computers, whatever they are learning is being learned at a "higher level"—meaning beyond the level of simple factual recall. As a society we have become so complacent about computers that most adults never question whether their use is appropriate for children. But there is a body of good quality literature that addresses that question, and brings some issues to the forefront. Unfortunately, much of that literature is frowned upon by those who have some particular interest in the computer technology world. But in the technology question, two simple facts remain. First, it is almost as though to question the use of technology is to have committed some sort of academic heresy. Second, the idea that the simple presence of technology indicates better and better learning does not come from educators—it comes from the computer industry.

How then can we assume that the quest for a population equipped with technological savvy goes beyond the bounds of common reason? The literature and anecdotal observation are inundated with reports of large school expenditures supporting technology and its use to the exclusion of seemingly more critical expenditures. Drs. Dale and Bonnie Johnson are distinguished scholars who have contributed significantly to the profession of teacher preparation. Recently, they embarked on a project that should be the envy of professional educators everywhere when they took unpaid leaves of absence from their university positions and spent an entire school year teaching elementary school in a very poor rural area in northern Louisiana (Johnson and Johnson 2002b). Their book, *High Stakes: Children, Testing, and Failure in American Public Schools* (2002a), criticized many current practices that are essentially being legislated, but among other things took this technological mind-set to task. The Johnsons were appalled that while teaching in a poor school with no heat and no running hot water, those in charge managed to find the funds to support an $85,000 software program to provide drill and practice for high-stakes standardized testing. In a similar vein, Baines (1997) states,

> Despite the conundrums over funding for education and the state and local initiatives against raising taxes, expenditures for technology have soared. Over the course of five years in the school district in which I lived and taught, the number of students per classroom ballooned, budgets for textbooks and supplies were slashed, and plans were shelved for capital improvements to deteriorating buildings and for the construction of a new school. Yet new computers were purchased for every classroom in every school in the district, along with a number of videodisc players. Shortly after their purchase, several of the videodisc players became disabled and were moved into storage, where they have remained, gathering dust. Meanwhile, several classrooms were left with 20-year-old textbooks or no textbooks at all. (492)

Clearly, those in charge in our profession must come to some consensus and establish some specific boundaries regarding the use of technology and its place in our business. Likewise, those who make such instructional decisions must recognize technology as a tool to be used when appropriate. In the business of renovating homes, power screwdrivers and pneumatic nail guns are excellent tools to have on hand. However, it would be foolish to discard a regular screwdriver or hammer because sometimes they do the job far better and more efficiently. As such, the educational leaders who push for technology over all else need to become literate about the good and bad. Bernardo (1996) argues the point of technology use and instructional priorities:

> The jump from the classics to computer skills that will help "survival in the real world" is perhaps the key to the problem. As essential as computer skills are becoming, isn't there something wrong with the picture? Even with ac-

quisition of the 3R's and knowledge of U.S. history and geography, what will computer skills accomplish without the user's having been exposed to the great IDEAS [emphasis in original] that had created the modern world? This is what made our founding fathers capable of pinpointing "Life, Liberty and the Pursuit of Happiness" as the ultimate goal of a civilized society. Will computer skills help young people to grasp the meaning and importance of this goal? As one teacher in the poll pointed out, "Schools are trying to do the parents' job and, in some cases, [neglecting] the school's job of teaching a body of knowledge and thought needed to have thinking, educated people. If we valued the classics and history and advanced math and science, and gave those kids those concepts so that they would be thinking and knowledgeable, they would learn about computers later." As Chester Finn observed concerning the poll, "I think teachers have been brainwashed by the political-correctness crowd to think that anything associated with the 'classics' is claimed as 'dead, white European male' imperialist." Vice President Gore gave a general summary of what has occurred so far by stating that the on-line revolution "will forever change the way we live, learn, work and communicate." We must now stop and ask, "Can computers really improve the quality of people's lives without interfering with the inalienable rights of Life, Liberty and the Pursuit of Happiness?" (4)

There has been a great deal written in recent years concerning the aftereffects of child development that are directly linked to the presence of computers in their lives. The very nature of a computer is that the work is done one person at a time. As such, extended computer use at an early age is thought to influence a child's socialization. Also, it is thought that dependence on the computer, and the often-unnatural manner in which the eyes are expected to move, tends to slow down the natural processes in learning to read.

CURRENT PROGRESSIVE MOVEMENTS
AND ORGANIZATIONS

It is clearly established in both the theoretical literature and anecdotal observation of current practices that the progressive ideas—or those claiming to be progressive—dominate the educational thinking of today. There are several very current trends that are having some major influences on

the design and workings of the schools. Although not necessarily speci-
fied as such, these movements are very progressive in nature because of
the positions put forth, the teaching and learning behaviors that are
demonstrated or demanded, and the desired outcomes that are expressed.
There are many educational leaders who express serious concern that such
programs and practices that blatantly exemplify progressive ideas to the
exclusion of any other are presented in such a manner as to be presumed
the ultimate and unquestionably desired. Let us examine some of the current programs, movements, practices, and organizations that should be of
concern, or at least questionable, to the informed practitioner.

National Board for Professional Teaching Standards (NBPTS)

In educational and political circles, the point is often argued, with good intentions, that teaching must become recognized as professional in the same
vein as medical, legal, and business professionals. While the idea of a national level of teacher certification has been discussed for many years, the
National Board for Professional Teaching Standards (NBPTS) was formed in
1987 by a group of very well-intended educators. The board was formed in
an effort to both raise the standards of teaching professionals as well as to
grant an additional level of licensure to teachers in much the same manner as
physicians choose a specialty beyond their very generic medical education
leading to their doctor of medicine degree. Since that time, thousands of
teachers across the nation have pursued the supposedly rigorous standards of
the National Board. School systems across the country boast of the persons
in their employ who have attained such status as well as university colleges
of education and their graduates. And while most assume that meeting the
supposedly rigorous standards of the National Board creates an assurance of
professionalism and quality, there are facts surrounding the certification
process and outcomes that are typically unknown by the general public.

First, the National Board for Professional Teaching Standards bases its entire premise on five very broad standards that simply cannot be separated from
the extremes in progressive ideology. These five very broad standards are:

1. Teachers are committed to students and their learning.
2. Teachers know the subjects they teach and how to teach those subjects
   to students.

3. Teachers are responsible for managing and monitoring student learning.
4. Teachers think systematically about their practice and learn from experience.
5. Teachers are members of learning communities.

On the surface it can hardly be argued that these five standards are certainly desirable attributes in what we expect of teachers at any level. Likewise, a cursory read-through will cause most experienced educators to briefly reflect and think, "These are probably things good teachers do anyway." But as we discuss further, we will see how the supposed simplicity of the standards is quite misleading and generally not in keeping with what is supposedly the mission of the National Board.

Next, during the first fifteen years of its existence, the NBPTS has been supported by a great deal of tax money—in excess of $200 million at the time of this writing (2004)—with virtually no oversight or accountability that ordinarily would come with the receipt of federal dollars. Almost any other organization in receipt of that much tax money would of necessity have some sort of plan of evaluation in place before such dollars were expended. This apparently has not been the case with NBPTS.

Unlike graduate study in a university or the completion of other professional programs, the process of National Board certification is not intended to be an experience in professional development, to refine teaching techniques, to improve one's existing practices in any way, or to bring something new to the person's classroom. Unlike some of the specialty training in medicine or law, National Board certification is supposedly a process by which the best teachers are identified as meeting what NBPTS has determined to be the highest standards of pedagogical delivery and professional thought (Podgursky 2001a). National Board standards do touch briefly on content, but it is clearly their intent that pedagogy is their focus. Essentially, National Board certification does not bring about any sort of *change* or *improvement* in the teacher's individual practices, nor is the practitioner's professional perspective expected to change. The certification process simply measures or identifies those who report beliefs and have graphically demonstrated practices that parallel the beliefs of NBPTS.

It should concern some leaders greatly that those who do actually attain National Board certification consistently exhibit certain tendencies. Current information indicates that those attaining the certification tend to be predominantly white females who currently teach in the very desirable, middle-class, predominantly white suburban school systems (Bond 1998b; Moore 1999). It is generally known that students from such school systems present far fewer social problems than the urban and inner-city schools. It is also well known that students in such areas come to school with certain middle-class advantages that are known to influence student outcomes far more than anything that happens at school. It is well known that students from these areas and backgrounds are more easily served by the vague, progressive ideas that are purported by NBPTS. Additionally, according to Moore (1999), the teachers who attain National Board certification tend to possess the background to write about their teaching and teaching experiences in such a manner and to a degree as to find favor with the National Board. This information should truly call into question whether National Board standards are generally desirable or even applicable across the profession (Burroughs, Schwartz, and Hendricks-Lee 2000). Burroughs (2001) states,

> Irvine and Fraser (1998) have argued that African American teachers may use a "culturally specific pedagogical style" that they call "warm demanders." They argue that teachers who are warm demanders may appear to be more teacher-centered than NBPTS standards allow. Bond (1998a) has suggested that "cultural markers" in African American discourse styles may affect how NBPTS assessors score texts written by African American candidates. (231)

The glaring evidence that NBPTS is so focused in progressive ideology brings forth another point. It is well known from years of research that children from disadvantaged backgrounds tend to fare better when taught via more traditional, teacher-centered methods (Chall 2000; Delpit 1996). By their own admission, certification by the National Board is generally identifying and documenting what NBPTS considers to be the "best practices," not changing your practices (J. Isingberg, visiting scholar for NBPTS, personal communication, January 11, 2003). Since we know of the strong tendency by NBPTS to view progressive, child-centered practices as the desired, then teachers who, of necessity, must teach in other ways would seem to be automatically eliminated as a candidate for board certification. This would bring forth two questions:

1. Is it possible that a relationship exists between the socioeconomic status of the population being served and the likelihood of a teacher earning board certification?
2. Is it possible or even likely that the certification of teachers in this manner actually hinders the quality of education for those children who are at a disadvantage?

But of critical importance is the fact that, fifteen years after the establishment of the National Board, there is no empirical data to suggest or support that children taught by the teachers identified by NBPTS as superior achieve any more than those taught by non–board-certified teachers (Holland 2002a, 2002b). This causes one to seriously question the amount of money spent on this idea or the emphasis on such ideas.

In fairness to the National Board, I will assert that within the past year (2003) the National Board has called for proposals to complete empirical research on their programs and their people. Obviously, the board wants to be recognized as legitimate and wants real and credible data to support its work (Archer 2002)—but at the time of this writing, no such credible data exists. NBPTS apparently does not wish to have student performance data used as a measure of board-certified teacher effectiveness. It is interesting to note that the National Board has commissioned and funded twenty-two studies, but only two are empirical. All others are quite descriptive in nature that, while beautifully conceived and executed, won't tell us much more than we already know.

Podgursky (2001b) refers to a report released by the National Board (Bond, Jaeger, Smith, and Hattie 2000) that compares a sample of teachers who had earned National Board certification to those who had not. Podgursky points out significant flaws in the research design:

> No study, however, has ever shown that National Board–certified teachers are any better than other teachers at raising student achievement. Nothing has changed with the release of this report. The National Board's research rejected the use of student test scores as a measure of teacher performance, claiming, "It is not too much of an exaggeration to state that such measures have been cited as a cause of all of the nation's considerable problems in educating our youth. . . . It is in their uses as measures of individual teacher effectiveness and quality that such measures are particularly inappropriate." . . . The shortcomings of this study, the paucity of independent research on the National

Board, and the large investments being made by states in rewarding National Board–certified teachers highlight the need for a rigorous and arm's-length cost-benefit study of the National Board. (4, 6)

The assertions made in this report really should come as no surprise to the thinking public. After all, those employed by a particular fast-food restaurant chain will likely prepare food in the manner prescribed by the restaurant than those employed elsewhere.

Of interesting note is that one recent study has evoked the furor of many proponents of NBPTS. John Stone (2002) completed a small study in Tennessee that was apparently the first formal research done to actually compare student achievement of children taught by National Board–certified teachers and those taught by non–board-certified teachers. While the sample was admittedly small (the State of Tennessee has a very limited number of National Board–certified teachers), his findings indicated there is no significant difference in the achievement or performance of the children taught by nationally certified teachers. Part of the research included the use of "value-added assessment," the value of which is still unclear. Naturally, the methods, sampling, and other details came under serious attack by the NBPTS and other supporters of the board, but was praised by various social science scholars. However, one fact remains: Although the study was small—and one study is hardly conclusive—Dr. Stone was apparently the first researcher to call the certification by the National Board into question and back up his findings with real numbers, not descriptive comparisons. It will be interesting to see what further research comes forth as a result of this.

One other matter of concern is the reward and recognition for having completed National Board certification. When the National Board certification is completed, the certification is active for ten years. Many states pay teachers a stipend for having completed the certification, and in some states (Louisiana, for example) the National Board stipend is as much as $5,000 to $7,500 annually, for the life of the certificate (ten years). Even if the teacher moves into administration, they are still paid the stipend on top of their administrative salary, which seriously calls into question the idea of "keeping the best and brightest in the classrooms." I am among those who are greatly concerned that states will so generously reward teachers for completing this certification that is so focused in one direction—specifically, the progressive ideologies—and apparently disregard any other mode of professional development or any other legitimate graduate study. When a teacher attends a university and engages in traditional graduate study that broadens his or her perspective and culminates in the conferral of a master's or doctoral degree, their financial remuneration from the state may be as little as $500 annually. Again, we see the dominance of progressive ideals attached to some serious financial rewards with no clear evidence that such ideals are clearly superior to any other or that such produces a better outcome (Wright 1990). At this point, it is not unfair to state that there is not a body of empirical evidence to support the notion that National Board–certified teachers perform any better (Rotberg, Hatwood-Futrell, and Lieberman 1998) while there is a plethora of evidence to support that those holding an advanced degree do.

The dominant presence and complacent acceptance of National Board standards as the unerring ideal is finding its way into higher education as well. As the seemingly uninformed popularity of NBPTS continues to grow, institutions that train teachers are beginning to acquiesce as well. There are many colleges of education who are attempting to align their program standards to those of the National Board in an attempt to give their graduates an advantage should they decide to pursue national certification. Some universities are offering graduate courses focused entirely on the preparation of the documents for the National Board assessment. I would think many people would be concerned that such courses were paid for by tuition exemption dollars. We don't find such extravagant treatment in other professions, particularly when the process in question has not been shown to be of benefit.

But there is one additional issue with NBPTS that should concern practitioners more than any other. Much of the working and practice of the NBPTS seems to operate in a veil of secrecy. The criterion by which a candidate's work is judged does not seem to be readily available for the general public to see. There apparently are no written criteria to state that "if you do this, you will be granted national certification." According to Bond (1998b), "No standardized procedures exist for detecting measurement deficiencies in complex performance assessment, and so they must be developed" (212). There are writings and reports of individuals whose experiences, practices, and methods should easily fall into the acceptable category according to the five general standards of NBPTS, but did not for reasons that were never made clear (Nehrig 2001). After the serious financial expenditure as well as expenditure of professional and personal time, candidates whose work is not accepted seem to have little recourse because the criteria for acceptance is so vague and, according to Petrosky (1994), candidate feedback is often "canned" (36). In keeping with what are unquestioned scholarly practices, what should be public information about pass rates, demographics, and so forth seem to be carefully shielded from the public (Burroughs 2001). It would likely cause national certification to be seen in an entirely different light should the board release information concerning the ethnicity, educational background, and level of experience of those who do make it past the supposedly rigorous standards of NBPTS. It is a great matter of concern that such questionable behaviors of the board are so visible, being supported by many public dollars with generally no oversight or accountability, and with no clear evidence that the person certified by the NBPTS produces a better end product. In a study of the validity of the National Board certification, Pool, Ellett, Schiavone, and Carey-Lewis (2001) state,

> In the current era of increased educational accountability, reform and professionalization of teaching, teacher credentialing and compensation are likely to continue as topics of considerable discussion and debate. The results reported here suggest that education policymakers and others should move cautiously in endorsing and investing in credentials-based pay incentives solely grounded in passing new forms of national assessment. Assessments like the NBPTS certification process can tell us much about the personal commitment of selected teachers to strive to obtain professionally endorsed national credentials that have high symbolic (and economic) value. However, there appear to be no assurances that attaining these credentials guarantees quality and learning environments in everyday practice. What seems needed are newer models of credentialing and accountability for teachers that better integrate the roles of state licensing, local district evaluations, national certification, and continuous growth, with career development paths, options, and incentives. (46–47)

American Board for the Certification of Teaching Excellence (ABCTE)

It is often argued that a little competition can be a healthy thing, and the furthering of the social sciences is probably no exception to this idea. Although the credibility of the NBPTS is still not quite clear, the board has held a position of monopoly until recently. Another organization, the American Board for the Certification of Teaching Excellence (ABCTE)—known quite generically as the American Board—was formed in Washington, D.C., with similar aspirations, but from a slightly different perspective. It is apparent from the literature and the current work of the American Board that they are intended to be both a manner of identifying teaching excellence as well as earning a portable teaching credential. ABCTE (2001) is a much newer organization than NBPTS (1987), but at the time of this writing has been appropriated $5 million by the government for the development of their credentialing processes.

National Board certification is clearly intended to be a supplement to whatever state licensure the teacher already holds. American Board certification, however, offers candidates from different backgrounds some choices. The American Board is offering what is called "passport" certification, which in short is quite comparable to many of the alternative or "practitioner" certification programs in existence around the country. Just like the general rule in alternative certification programs, candidates must hold an accredited bachelor's degree in some field before attempting to earn their teaching credential. But, like the National Board, the American Board offers experienced teachers the opportunity to upgrade their credentials by demonstrating teaching excellence through subject-matter exams and the demonstration of student achievement.

The credentialing process being designed by ABCTE does not involve videotaping of lessons or the preparation of portfolios, but instead involves objective testing of both content and professional pedagogy. This idea pleases many traditional thinkers but evokes the anger of the more progressive thinkers. In the political rhetoric and squabbling between the two organizations and their respective missions, we hear such remarks as "With ABCTE, you just take a test and you're a teacher." But that argument is quite shortsighted, as there really is no way a person would be able to pass a test of pedagogical knowledge without having studied such at some level. So the argument that the credentialing process of ABCTE is a shortcut or "quickie" method to teacher certification is quite unfair and seriously misinformed.

I recently had the opportunity to spend several hours with leaders from NBPTS and ABCTE over the same weekend. With the onset of the No

Child Left Behind legislation, and the definition of a "highly qualified teacher" not particularly clear, it is interesting to note that federal leaders have already determined ABCTE's practice as identifying "highly qualified" educators. While a couple of states have accepted and are espousing ABCTE's methods and ideals, states are not offering the same financial remuneration as for National Board certification.

Recently, a media frenzy erupted when the American Board was preparing to field test its first round of exams; test information was leaked to the public, making all the preparation to that point virtually useless. Over a period of several weeks, accusations flew and political rumblings abounded. We should wait with curiosity to see how this professional battle plays out.

PRAXIS

The PRAXIS series is a product of the Educational Testing Service (ETS) of Princeton, New Jersey, and has been in use for many years. Originally titled the National Teacher Exam, the exam consisted of three general parts (general knowledge, professional knowledge, communication skills) followed by specialty exams in various teaching fields, including administration. The format of the exam changed considerably a few years ago to include a writing sample that is scored by teams of readers. The scope of the exam has changed over the years, but essentially there are still three general parts to the exam, which are taken early in a person's teacher-training program. The specialty areas are taken close to graduation. The exam that is called PRAXIS I is the test of preprofessional and writing skills. The PRAXIS II series consists of the specialty area exams. PRAXIS III will eventually be a set of exams that are intended to be a uniform and standardized tool for evaluating a new teacher's performance.

It is of concern to many educational leaders that so many states are becoming so dependent upon and using the PRAXIS exam as the determining criteria for admission to and graduation from a teacher-training program. This level of concern is twofold. Of primary concern is that one test holds such a prominent place in the certification of so many teachers. Of equal concern is that the focus of a licensing exam for so many states is so blatantly focused in the direction of progressive ideals, and the apparent mind-set that anything else is unacceptable.

Why, then, should the foregoing be of such concern to practitioners and educational leaders? Three questions must be asked:

1. Is there any empirical data that would support that a "high" or "passing" score on the PRAXIS is related to a person's success in a teacher-training program?
2. Is there any empirical data that would support that a "high" or "passing" score on the PRAXIS is related to a person's subsequent success as a teacher?
3. If such data does exist, was the data gathered and compiled by anyone not affiliated with ETS?

It is fair to assert that the answers to the above three questions are "no, no, and no." As such, it is argued that ETS has a great deal of influence on what is taught in colleges of education, what is taught in the schools, and also how textbook and computer software companies respond to the dominant thinking. Cunningham (2001) states,

> I can't speak for what is happening in the 12 states not using PRAXIS, but what this means is that ETS through this test is now able to exert considerable control over the curriculum of schools of education. Schools have no choice but to teach what ETS says is important. At least on the Elementary Education Curriculum Instruction and Assessment, ETS has made a clear and almost total commitment to progressive education. Teaching items are devoted to whole language, language experience, reading/writing workshops, etc. They promote a balanced approach to reading, which means that although they believe in whole language they are willing to concede that phonemic awareness is also important. Beginning readers will certainly learn it though osmosis or something. Math is completely NCTM [National Council of Teachers of Mathematics] based. Science is strictly inquiry-based. The distracters or wrong answers tend to refer to direct instruction practices such as requiring correct spelling, using tests, memorization, etc. (1)

Obviously, the progressive focus cannot be seen in exams that focus on a body of content. Only the exams that focus on the pedagogy can be said to focus on this direction. There are exams that purportedly measure and assess "Principles of Learning and Teaching," and it is not only at the elementary level of this testing program that we find such a strong influence of progressive ideals. To illustrate the progressive focus in the design of PRAXIS exams, let us examine some questions from currently available online registration for the PRAXIS Education in the Elementary School. Consider the following example:

> In teaching regrouping with two-digit numbers for the first time to a third-grade class, which of the following would provide the best initial means for a teacher to demonstrate the concept?
>
> A. Manipulative materials
> B. Illustrations drawn on the chalkboard
> C. A chart of sets of objects
> D. Examples from an appropriate mathematics textbook
> E. A written model of how regrouping is recorded

The answer choice of ETS is answer A. Each of the other responses, however, is a perfectly acceptable mode of instruction for the right group of children at the right time. In keeping with progressive ideologies, however, there are two reasons this would be the answer of choice. First, the idea of manipulatives—something concrete that can be touched, felt, explored, and is concrete in nature—is very much a part of progressive, child-centered ideals. Second, all other answer choices, while appropriate for some children at some time, are focused in the direction of (or at least can be interpreted as) teacher directed—the teacher providing the new information from his or her role as the force behind the learning. Purely progressive ideas and teacher-centered practices generally don't mix.

Let us look at another example:

> Of the following, the best way to present the contributions of women of both the past and the present would be to
>
> A. invite important community resource people to speak on the roles of women in the workplace
> B. present and discuss case studies that focus on women's rights
> C. solicit classroom involvement by the students' parents
> D. incorporate into as many subject areas as possible information about the accomplishments of women
> E. include at each grade level a social studies unit on famous women

The answer choice of ETS is answer D. Again, all the other answer choices are perfectly acceptable classroom practices and it is logical to assume that each would significantly contribute to the children's understanding and appreciation of the role women have played in the development of this nation. There is one word that should provide a hint as to the answer of choice: incorporate. Progressive ideals insist that subject matter is not broken into separate disciplines but instead that all subjects are integrated and incorporated into all the other subjects. There are two reasons why the other four answer choices would be rejected by the test-makers of ETS:

1. All the other answer choices fall into categories that can be considered teacher-centered—the antithesis of the progressive ideology as "teacher as guide on the side, not sage on the stage." All the other answer choices involve an experienced, authoritative adult bringing information to children.
2. All the answer choices, but particularly choice E, involve the delivery of instruction or new information in an isolated format, seemingly separate from other disciplines—or at least as an isolated presentation.

I would add at this point that it is quite conceivable that answer choice E may very well provide for a far better level of instruction than that of answer choice D. Incorporating as much information as one can manage into existing instruction is not an inherently bad idea. However, doing so certainly creates the opportunity for what information is incorporated to be of a hit-or-miss nature rather than a planned, sequential set of instructional lessons. Providing the instruction via answer choice E may not fit as nicely into the progressive ideals, but can certainly provide a more fluid and coherent experience than tiny pieces of seemingly trivial information tossed into the regular instruction.

Let us look at one other example of the dominance of progressive ideals in the PRAXIS series:

In the early years of elementary school, the emphasis of science teaching should be on the development of:

A. knowledge about scientists and their accomplishments
B. ability in the areas of science in which the students express an interest
C. a broad background of science facts and figures
D. an understanding of the structure or conceptual framework of science
E. a repertoire of processes that the students can use to interpret their environment

The answer choice of ETS is answer E. As before, all other answer choices are perfectly acceptable classroom practices in the right circumstance with the right group of students and utilized for the right reasons. As before, all the "wrong" choices fall into the categories that cannot be considered progressive or child-centered as interpreted by ETS (in this example, answer choice B is somewhat questionable). Each of these choices tends to focus on a collective body of information that all children should know whereas the desired answer fits nicely with the ideal described earlier. Progressive teaching methods prefer to develop a group of generic problem-solving skills (which many consider fictitious) that presumably will allow the children to learn by discovery anything they would ever need to know.

But the preponderance of progressive ideas does not stop with the multiple-choice sections of the PRAXIS. There are subtests entitled "Principles of Teaching and Learning" for various grade levels (K–4, 5–9, 7–12). Each of the tests contains a lengthy passage to be read that describes a classroom situation, the practices of the teacher, the behaviors of the students, and the material being taught. Following the passage are several questions that ask the student to analyze or critique the teaching situation. It is not hard to ascertain from the wording of the questions that the focus of the inquiry is slanted in favor of the progressive, child-centered answer and obviously expressing bias against anything that remotely resembles teacher-centered instruction.

It is too easy and convenient to overutilize the PRAXIS score as part of the criterion for teacher certification. As states have begun to report student passing-rate data to the public as some flawed means of accountability, universities are understandably under pressure to produce students who pass the exam. Unfortunately, however, several universities have come under fire from ETS for using the PRAXIS exam as a requirement for graduation from their program, when such was clearly never the intention of ETS.

National Council for the Accreditation of Teacher Education (NCATE)

The National Council for the Accreditation of Teacher Education (NCATE) is a professional organization whose stated mission is to bring the highest uniform standards to colleges of education across the nation. The organization was founded in 1954 (Stone 2000b) and has undergone various revisions and changes over the years, but the original intent was to unify and bring some consistency to teacher training and the work of colleges of teacher education. Prior to that time, any kind of oversight in teacher training had been quite fragmented and varied from state to state and university to university. Since its inception, NCATE has been the premier accrediting organization, accrediting about 500 of the 1,300 or so colleges of education in the country. NCATE has managed to align itself with some state departments of education; 28 states have adopted NCATE standards as the state standards, thereby essentially mandating NCATE's philosophies and ideals with no regard for any other (Stone 2000b; Blair 2001).

There was a time when recognition and accreditation by NCATE was thought of as a modest effort by an individual college of education to demonstrate its willingness to show such to the public. It was during this time that meeting NCATE standards was quite similar to meeting accreditation standards of the six regional accreditation agencies of colleges and universities or other options that would accredit other academic disciplines. It is unfortunate that this is not the case today.

In 1987 NCATE rewrote a set of standards that stayed in place until 2000, when the standards were rewritten to focus on performance-based standards rather than the previous curriculum-based standards (Stone 2000b). Previously, the determination of "excellent" had been the elements of "input" into a teacher-education program. Such inputs included faculty qualifications and experience, library resources, and unique learning opportunities afforded by the individual institutions. Under the new standards, excellence is determined by certain competencies to be demonstrated by the program graduates during the early part of their teaching career. Those educational writers who are critical of the standards movement in general will likewise be critical of the NCATE 2000 standards. Stone (2001) states,

Spurred by growing dissatisfaction with the quality of teacher training, NCATE recently proposed a change from curriculum-based accreditation standards to ones based on the competencies displayed by aspiring teachers (National Council for the Accreditation of Teacher Education 1999). The new standards express concern for improved teacher knowledge and they say that student learning is teaching's most important goal. However, the educational priorities they promote are the same, i.e. social idealism first, student achievement second. The only real difference is that the new standards assess whether aspiring teachers have mastered the pedagogical orthodoxy whereas the old standards assessed whether the training program's curriculum was properly infused with orthodoxy. (2)

Stone is not alone in his concern that those who align with NCATE are far more adept at writing about what they believe to be good teaching than to demonstrate it.

The NCATE Unit Standards for 2002 are as follows:

Standard 1—Candidate Knowledge, Skills, and Dispositions
Standard 2—Assessment System and Unit Evaluation
Standard 3—Field Experiences and Clinical Practice
Standard 4—Diversity
Standard 5—Faculty Qualifications, Performance, and Development
Standard 6—Unit Governance and Resources

It would certainly stand to reason that those concerned with the blatant preponderance of progressive ideals would look cautiously at the six-standard framework upon which NCATE accreditation is based. These standards are so broad as to be realistically interpreted in many, many different ways. Standard 1 does vaguely mention the necessity of the mastery of a body of content, but the wording of "skills" and "dispositions" is open to really generous interpretation, particularly as it relates to the teacher's personal perspective on social and ethical matters. There are many educational scholars who express grave concern over teacher-candidate's interpretations and "dispositions." Disposition is loosely defined as "what one thinks relative to his or her personal behaviors." It is not possible to measure what individuals think except through some sort of survey or "disposition scale," which is a weak measure by any standard or design. Such measures are only a quantification of how the person *reports* his or her beliefs.

Somehow, in the midst of all the tenuous, academic discussion about teacher education standards, alignment of standards, and all, one point never seems to come forth: If only about one-third of the colleges of education in this country are aligned with and accredited by NCATE, then what is the big deal? Although NCATE, like NBPTS, does not like to release some data to the public, it is not difficult to figure out certain things. The institutions that have aligned themselves with NCATE tend to fall into one of two categories:

1. Regional or state-supported universities with teacher education being one of the larger programs for which NCATE accreditation is a serious marketing tool;
2. Teacher training institutions in twenty-eight of the fifty states that have chosen to align their standards with NCATE.

When an institution is seeking accreditation from NCATE, the process is arduous and time-consuming. It is so labor intensive as to unreasonably impose on faculty time and energy. It is a frequent complaint that faculty must neglect their teaching responsibilities in favor of the extensive record keeping and documentation that helps an institution find favor with NCATE. Larger institutions that can afford additional clerical help during the NCATE preparation do not seem to feel the strain on instructional time as much as the smaller institutions who must force the burden onto their faculty. I find it interesting to note that several of the most prestigious universities in the country, each of which is noted for contributions to the world of educational research and practice and is the academic home of some of the country's greatest scholars, are not accredited by NCATE. Harvard University, Teachers College of Columbia University, Princeton, and New York University are not accredited by NCATE (Columbia is seeking accreditation, but only because the state of New York is insisting on it) (Vergari and Hess 2002). Is it that these institutions possibly don't meet the exacting standards of NCATE or do these institutions have more important things to do?

There is much current literature indicating that colleges of education are becoming increasingly disillusioned—sometimes outright disgusted—with NCATE and the seemingly unreasonable demands that seem to want every college of education bearing this seal to be a carbon copy of another. Laboriously bowing to "what NCATE wants to see" has been compared to purchasing a franchise. When one buys into the franchise of a major

fast-food restaurant, then everything the restaurant does must be accountable to whatever rules the franchise has chosen to impose.

The Teacher Education Accreditation Council (TEAC)

For the past several years, another organization has been gradually inching
its way into the national accreditation scene—the Teacher Education Accreditation Council (TEAC). TEAC was formed by a group of smaller-
college presidents and other interested persons to allow smaller schools to
have some choices about accreditation that may not be as burdensome for
smaller programs. The intent was to be an organization of the same status
and prestige as NCATE, but would be more useful to smaller programs that
often have little in common with large universities. Bradley (1998) states,
"The alternative accrediting effort is founded on the opposing belief that
states should retain full control over approving teacher education programs
and licensing teachers, and that accreditation should remain voluntary and
separate from licensure. TEAC's founders also intend for college and university presidents to play a major role in governing the new council" (22).

Unlike NCATE, TEAC does not intend to accredit entire schools of education, but instead places seals of approval on individual programs
within the school—thus personalizing the accrediting process and result.
It is argued that prior to 2000, NCATE standards were all about program
inputs (quality of faculty, library resources, publications, etc.) with little
regard for what students did after exiting the program. When TEAC began their initial work, NCATE rose to the challenge. But the bottom line
in the NCATE/TEAC squabble is that smaller schools simply cannot bear
the burden and expense that NCATE has come to demand (Blair 2001).

But of greater concern—and what should alarm the public—is that there
really is not a body of compelling evidence to support the notion that
NCATE-trained teachers perform any better on licensing exams or student
achievement (Vergari and Hess 2002). Performance-based standards are
not as outwardly visible as the previous program-input standards. Consequently, since the implementation of the 2000 standards, NCATE has been
increasingly dependent upon hard data to support the claims of colleges of
education. It is not at all unreasonable for those of us who have been
through the NCATE experience and support NCATE's mission to ask for
that same compelling evidence that what we have done has made us better.

Animal Farm Revisited

There is much about the workings of school reform that closely parallels the working of the mythical Animal Farm. Such parallelisms include the drive for efficiency becoming a narcissistic power struggle in which preferential agendas are supported at the expense of all concerned. Additionally, by keeping the constituents ignorant, they can be more easily controlled. This has certainly been the case in many states and school systems across the country.

In the next chapter, we look at some problems that exist in the establishment of a professional knowledge base within our profession. When the boundaries of professional knowledge are not clear, it is quite easy for those in the profession to be misled by information that is inherently flawed or is being selectively chosen to support a particular agenda.

Chapter Four

Broken Promises: Why Progressive Education Has Failed to Deliver

Dewey's attempts to dissociate himself from vulgar interpretations of progressivism did not help him much for his name is closely linked to progressivism, even in its vulgar interpretations.

— T. Englund, 2000

It is little wonder that society at large has so little respect for public education and all that goes on in the name thereof. First, it is well known that those who teach are generally considered the less able of society and have always been assumed to be so. We know that professionals who provide services to children and youth are generally dismissed or looked upon unfavorably by those of the profession who provide those same services to adults. There is a misguided mind-set that in the fields of medicine, education, psychology, or the ministry a lesser degree of training or expertise is needed by those who provide services to children and youth (D. Buford, editor, World Aflame Publications, personal communication, July 4, 2002). Second, the mass media, the means by which probably more than 99 percent of all adult Americans get their information, seldom has a kind thing to say about the schools and their efforts. Compliments on a job well done or an exemplary school or school system that did well (while staring at some precarious odds) do not make stimulating conversation and certainly don't make for good political agendas. But if progressive education—the methods, the desired outcomes, and the client base to be served—is such a desired end and anything other than progressive efforts are considered unacceptable, how then can we entertain the idea that progressive education might have failed? Are the ideas bad ones? Is the theory inherently flawed?

Have theories been misapplied? Is it possible that those in charge are absolute nincompoops? Is the possibility of a system of public education that will serve the needs of every single child, regardless of background or handicapping condition, merely a pipe dream? I have argued adamantly that, throughout all the years of ideological wars, teachers have only done whatever was asked of them (Norris 2002). But the answer to this unwinnable argument is . . . it depends on whom you ask. Ayers (1990) makes the following point:

> While progressive educational thought as developed by John Dewey (1900; 1902; 1916; 1938) and as actualized in the work of thousands of thinkers and practitioners over the last hundred years (see Schubert, 1986) has a long and noble history, it also has been much misunderstood and maligned. Contrary to popular belief, however, progressivism has never taken hold in American public schools in any massive way. Sadly, progressivism is a tradition much more of thought than of practice. Occasional examples of a fully articulated progressive practice in individual schools or classrooms exist, but the progressive takeover of the schools does not exist as suggested by alarmists from the dominant traditional and social behaviorist camps who casually blame progressivism, by which they mean "do-nothingism," for school failure (e.g., see Ravitch and Finn, 1987). (1)

Several years ago I interviewed a number of school personnel, including teachers, administrators, central office personnel, and even university professors, asking a prepared set of questions. Essentially, I asked why the progressive ideologies are the dominant force in public education. The most frequent response was similar in that progressive ideas came about as a well-intended effort at "leveling the playing field"—providing an educational opportunity that was practical, useful, and had generally been unavailable to the masses only a few years earlier. Unfortunately, the well-intended ideas had been taken to such an extreme as to become detrimental rather than beneficial. Well-meaning policymakers, often not from the same backgrounds as the children who are intended to be served by progressive education, have been unable to see that seldom can we force one size to fit all. But the problem really extends far beyond such a simplistic analysis. It really should come as no surprise that many of the early progressive educators made the same mistakes that are being made today. Many practices that continue to exist in the schools under the misguided notion of being "progressive" are clearly a series of misunderstandings about some very complex ideas. The bottom line here is that too many educational leaders, though well meaning in their focus, have simply tried to make progressive education into something it is not. Sclan (1990) states, "Many of the child-centered progressives turned Dewey's philosophy into a blind ideology which left its imprint on the field of education. Above all, they distorted Dewey's focus on the principles of 'interaction' and 'continuity' in defining 'educative experiences.' Alarmingly, the false ideology of education has become self-perpetuating" (1).

Likewise, Winter (1997) asserts that progressive education has been "borrowed from, misread, and maligned" (3). Winter states,

> For most of its defenders, progressive education is a meaningful, even powerful approach to teaching. Yet I have referred to it as an "endangered species," a philosophy whose growth is currently threatened. By threats, I don't have in mind schools with different approaches. We all know there are many fine avenues. It's not my goal to promote a "one way only" kind of thinking.... While many schools have adopted progressive language, terms such as "child-centered" and "active," "integrated" learning, bits and pieces of progressive practice, they may not be committed to the philosophy itself. There are many parents who prefer more easily defined rungs for their children's educational progress—pages, scores and the basics. (2)

Regardless of the merits of the controversy or on which side of the controversy one chooses to sit, it must be remembered that the early writers and theorists who brought forth this battle had clearly honest intentions of making public education a far more democratic process than it had ever been (Doll 1983). It is clear from the history of Dewey, Kilpatrick, the University of Chicago, and other pioneers that the progressive ideals came about in response to changes in society, what society was demanding, and a desirable vision of what can be accomplished. Working-class families were demanding an opportunity for the less privileged of society to have the option of some form of formal education that would have been unavailable, or even unthinkable, only a few years prior. Beane (1998) states,

> Yet despite the sad fate of the progressive movement, a persistent impulse that should not be disregarded ran deep among the great progressives. That impulse was the firm conviction that democracy is possible, that the democratic

way of life can be lived, and that our schools should and can bring democracy to life in the curriculum, in school governance, in community relations, and in the hearts and minds of young people. (8)

Eakin (2000) calls attention to the irony that the ideals of progressive education that were intended to serve the working-class individuals have done little to serve them. In fact, we know from a large and very credible body of research that it is the children of the upper-middle-class and generally affluent sector of society who are best served by the tenets and practices of progressive education (Chall 2000; Chall, Jacobs, and Baldwin 1990; Hirsch 1996; Iheoma 1997; Baker 1998). It is known unquestionably that the parents of this socioeconomic status tend to prefer this ideology to any other (Chall 2000). But in linking the theories of progressive education with the theories of developmentalism, Baker (1999) makes the following statement:

> Progress in education, and its extension into "teaching with a truly progressive spirit" around 1900, was tied to a social reform agenda that went beyond and yet held implications for the inscription of children under developmentalism (see Rice, 1893). Interestingly, there is no agreement in the present as to whether a progressive education *movement* [italics in original] ever existed. What have been identified instead are movements in which educators defined their work as "progressive." (814)

PERSISTENT CYCLES

Since WWII the schools have simply been unable to "catch up" to the sheer number of children they were expected to educate. Prior to that time, far fewer children attended school. When we look into the history of progressive education and make some comparisons of where, when, and how progressive education has "worked," we find some interesting similarities between the schools and school systems and various other striking parallelisms. In a previous book, I discussed the idea of the "dual school systems" (though neither the idea nor the terminology is my own) and what we find when duality exists. If we look at the supposedly distinguished, well-publicized cases of progressive education ideals that are reported as having been extremely successful, we find schools situated in neighborhoods that clearly reflect the ideas and mores of the middle class. In such success stories, we have not found schools with a majority of poor families, families struggling to meet the basic necessities of existence, or families that do not value and insist on the furthering of education within the family. We have found families who expect and appreciate a very refined way of life that is totally removed from the rough, vulgar side of life as is typically found in school systems where progressive education has not worked and perhaps never will.

In the schools where progressive ideals have not worked well, we find some glaring similarities. Years of research have shown clearly that a very strong link exists between the use, success, and acceptance of progressive ideals and a higher socioeconomic status of the children (Anyon 1980, 1981; Zilversmit 1993). Likewise, we have data supporting the idea that the strongest indicator of a child's school success is the educational level of the mother (Townsend 1988). Generally, when we find schools where progressive ideals have not worked well, we find poverty and disadvantaged ways of life. Where schools fail, we generally do not find affluence and community involvement.

It is an interesting paradox that the ideals of progressive education began as a manner in which to "level the playing field" between the affluent and less affluent. But today, progressive ideals seem to be the teaching method and ideology of choice of middle-class families (Chall 2000; Eberstadt 1999). Eberstadt (1999) states,

It appears, then, that progressive educational ideology has come full circle. Born near the turn of the century in hopes of raising the downtrodden up, it survives now as the ideology of choice of, by, and for the educational elite. . . . Indeed, it is increasingly recognized as such. Consider this comment by Nathan Glazer, writing last year in the *New Republic* of the sharply opposed visions of E. D. Hirsch and progressive educator Theodore Sizer. "The question of what's best for the classroom," Glazer concluded, "may simply be a matter of class—social class. In some schools, with some students, one can teach for understanding and depth. . . . For others—frankly and regrettably—there are not such things." Gardner, similarly, for all his talk of an "education for all human beings" notes that "for those disadvantaged children who do not acquire literacy in the dominant culture at home, such a prescribed curriculum [as that recommended by Hirsch and others] helps to provide a level playing field and to ensure that future citizens enjoy a common knowledge base." Progressivism, it appears, is not for the weak—or the backward, or the poor. (14)

CHILD-CENTEREDNESS MISAPPLIED

Anecdotal observation and an in-depth review of the current literature makes clear the fact that both early and contemporary progressive educators are remiss in a consensus on the meaning of "child-centered" education (Entwistle 1970; Postman and Weingartner 1973; Sclan 1990). It should concern many educational leaders and policymakers that so much misinformation exists in this area. When misinterpretations abound, the work of the educator is often trivialized. Black (2000) states,

> But educators, in their quest to create a shorthand that describes the process, have chosen phrases like "learning from children," "child-centered," or "children leading the curriculum" and thus have hampered adoption of progressive education. Such language generates perceptions of a lack of focus on politically important outcomes and too little control by adults. Nothing could be further from the truth. (39)

The terminology is attributed to Dewey, but this is disputed (see Chung and Walsh 2000). They state,

> The term "child-centered" has been prominent since the late 1800's. It remains central to the contemporary discourse of early childhood education (e.g., Shapiro 1983, Bredekamp 1987, Bredekamp and Rosegrant 1992, Bredekamp and Copple 1997). The term balances on many layers of complex and sometimes contradictory meanings forged over the years by competing interest groups, each appropriating the term for its own purposes. . . . Meanings are negotiated and changed across time. Part of the discourse of a given time, they carry baggage of discourse from earlier times and different places. We challenge the consensus use of *child-centered* [italics in original], particularly in early childhood education. (215–16)

Similarly, Postman and Weingartner (1973) state,

> The phrase is intended to communicate the simple and irreproachable idea that what you do in school ought to grow mostly out of the needs and interests of children. The problem is that some people have difficulty locating the line that separates responding to the needs of children from being destructively indulgent toward them. . . . Nonetheless, more than a few promising progressive schools have been ruined by the assumption that children can thrive in an environment in which they are treated exactly like adults. (139)

Unfortunately, it is quite common in our profession that complicated, desirable ideas that are attractive to mainstream thinking are often reduced to some idea consisting of nebulous boundaries that falter somewhere between a flawed interpretation and being outright wrong. As an example, several years ago a vice-principal came into my classroom to observe my teaching. When the vice-principal spoke to me later that day, she stated that she would like to see the classroom become more "child-centered." When I pushed her for clarification she stated, "Well, that just means that you need to have more pictures on the wall." That vice-principal, however, isn't the only misinformed professional. There are numerous writers who have addressed the question of child-centeredness being misapplied. Gallant (1973) states,

> A contemporary and popular definition of student-centered education probably would be in conflict with Dewey's original conception of the term, but might be consistent with the meaning which some of his ardent followers gave to it through their educational practices. . . . But like Rousseau, Dewey viewed education as the unfolding of the natural instincts and inclinations of the individual. Force-feeding of information which does not attend to the current needs and interests of the child is not likely to be beneficial or very productive. Both believed that adults are too prone to think of the education of children in terms of what adults should be able to accomplish, rather than in terms of what children need to know and do to live their lives at the present moment. Therefore, Dewey saw the child as the center of the educational process in the sense that it is he for whom education is intended. *He* becomes the basis for the selection and timing of subject matter and experiences. He is not *the* curriculum, nor does he intentionally and actively determine it, but it is planned in reference to him instead of to factors which are extraneous and unrelated to him. (411–12; italics in original)

As for child-centered ideology and its place in mainstream American education, Smith (1997) makes the following statement:

> Schools based on informal, child-centered ideas have never been mainstream in the American or any other system of education, but they have always been there. In the United States, they were much discussed and eagerly implemented during the progressive era of the 1920's and 1930's. In particular, private schools were set up specifically to embody progressive ideas, for example, the Shady Hill School in Cambridge, Massachusetts, the Hawken School in Cleveland, The School in Rose Valley near Philadelphia,

the Ethical Culture Schools in New York, among others. The period of the 1960's and 1970's, especially for those closely involved, is similarly remembered as a heady time, a time of excitement, progress, optimism, a sense of possibilities and new options for children. It seemed possible that schools—public and private alike—could actually make a positive difference in the lives of children and contribute to the search for alternatives to existing social institutions. Some educators even used words like *mission* and *the word* for the ideas and practices they were trying to spread. (372; italics in original)

Bonnie Grossen (1998), an advocate of content-focused instruction, calls the child-centered ideology into question by making note of some seriously misleading and obviously wrong assumptions. Grossen (1998) states,

A problematic assumption of child-directed practices is that a child cannot learn from instruction that is initiated and directed by a teacher. Instead, these practices assume that children's learning needs are best fulfilled by allowing each child to pursue his or her unique interests through play. . . . The idea that children often learn from the activities they initiate is perfectly reasonable. The idea that children should also have ample opportunities to take initiative is also acceptable. However, the idea that a teacher cannot possibly initiate and direct learning effectively requires closer examination. It may be that child-initiated and teacher-initiated learning both have an important place in education. (1)

Grossen (citing Walkerdine 1984 and Plowden 1967) goes on to argue that although the child-directed ideas are often attributed to Piaget, those ideas were around long before. According to Grossen, the ideas of Piaget were simply prominent at a convenient time when many leaders were trying to create some consistency in educational thought. Grossen continues to argue that the focus on the child, the child's needs, and the lack of focus on the content is clearly a by-product of Western civilization that is not seen in the Eastern civilizations, and their academic success rate is indicative of such (2).

Another component of the misapplied child-centered ideology is summed in a statement we hear quite often: "We teach children, not subjects." Again, the statement seems to exemplify a very humane and civilized method of providing for children and would seem to fit nicely with the ideas of Dewey. Unfortunately, the idea is seriously misleading because it only presents a portion of the bigger idea. Entwistle (1970, citing Connell 1963) challenges the flawed perspectives in this popular idea that seem to exemplify the study of the child rather than the study of a subject being passed on to the child (97). He states,

> Little remains to be added in criticism of this slogan. His argument is simply that if after a day spent in the classroom, and in response to the question "What have you been teaching?" you told your questioner, "Oh, nothing in particular, just children, that's all," he would be as nonplussed as if in reply to his question about what you had for dinner, you answered, "Oh nothing, I've just had dinner, but had nothing *for* dinner." What he could reasonably expect in reply to his question about your teaching would be an answer like, "mathematics," or "to be polite," or "how to play first base." He would be quite satisfied (at least that you were taking him seriously) if you had to confess that you had forgotten, or couldn't easily describe what you had taught. Your "nothing" might imply "nothing important," or indicate a disinclination to pursue the matter. Or "nothing" could mean that you had tried to teach arithmetic or how to swim but that your pupils had not succeeded in learning either of these things. . . . [One of the practical effects intended by the using the slogan] is that our teaching ought to be of skills and attitudes as well as mere information. (97; italics in original)

It is fair to say that the bottom line in the misapplication of child-centered is the consummately wrong notion that meeting a child's needs means creating some mythical environment whereby the child is never uncomfortable, frustrated, or unsuccessful in the short term (Norris 2003). Mirochnik (2003) makes the following point:

> What I find curious about theorists whose stories about educational practices fall into categories like critical pedagogy, Frierian education, constructivist teaching, and reconceptualist curriculum, is that so many who wave flags within these camps have not yet overcome Dewey's vocabulary of "child centered" teaching and learning. Instead of abandoning the need to define classroom practice in terms of some one center, many contemporary theorists, who ally themselves with the camps that I just mentioned, have tended to shift the location of authority away from the teacher's view of the world toward the way that children see it. (74)

Chung and Walsh (2000) summarize three general ways in which "child-centered" has been interpreted over the years:

1. The Froebelian ideology where the child is considered the center of the entire world;
2. The developmentalist ideology where the child is the center of all that is done at school;
3. The progressive ideology where the child is in charge of his or her activities and learning.

Clearly, each ideology overlaps to some extent, but none can ever single-handedly begin to serve the best interests of real children in real schools. Chung and Walsh (2000) make the following observation:

> Olson and Bruner (1996: 19) correctly call child-centered "a non-meaningful term at best." It has been a politically useful code word giving loosely affiliated groups a common identity. But the term has new and complex contradictory underlying assumptions about children and their learning and development that need to be brought to the forefront for the education of young children to be adequately addressed. (229)

Mirochnik (2003) brings forth an interesting perspective when he calls into question the idea that teaching and learning must have a "center." Apparently such an idea is derived from the extremist mind-set whereby some consider knowledge to be constantly discovered and rediscovered (evolving) while others consider it to be affirmed and reaffirmed (static). While the interpretations of the idea will always influence the manner in which instruction is designed and delivered, the ideology of child-centered must never be misinterpreted to mean that the teacher is anything other than an academic leader and authority, nor are the students their academic or authoritative equals.

OPEN EDUCATION

It is thought by many that the changes in thinking of the 1950s led to the social unrest of the 1960s (Feinberg and Odeshoo 2000). Probably the most drastic move in progressive directions came in the early to mid 1960s and became known as Open Education. Most thinking individuals would consider it unfortunate that many remember open education as an idea that is probably best forgotten (Smith 1997). Some recall classrooms with virtually no structure or obvious focus. Some recall schools in which it was encouraged for children to express themselves freely, even if such expression violated conventionally held norms about children's appropriate and inappropriate behaviors. Others recall school architecture that did not include walls. Bradley (1999) states,

> Never precisely defined, open education typically stressed giving children choices, and plenty of opportunities to experiment and get their hands dirty, in classrooms full of books, animals, and art supplies. Teachers monitor pupils' work, rather than dictate what they should study and learn. Curriculum and adult authority were played down. The process of learning—rather than knowledge acquired—was the goal. (32)

My own memory of open education recalls schools without walls—essentially, open warehouses where children were grouped for instruction separated by little more than portable bookshelves or chalkboards. I was an elementary school-age child during this time and my parents were undergraduate students in teacher education. As such, the unfolding movement and the likelihood of its permanence was a frequent topic of conversation in our home. During this time, the university that my parents attended built a large, state-of-the-art college of education with no walls. Deeply embedded in my memory is the serious effort my parents made to take us on a tour of the building and explain the significance of no walls. As an almost comical sidenote, some thirty years later I was a doctoral student attending a national conference and heard a professor from this university speak. Afterward at the reception, I spoke with the man and told him that I was a small child when that college of education was built, and I remembered it having no walls. The man laughed and remarked that when builders attempted to subsequently build walls where walls were not intended to be, the lights and air-conditioning never worked.

It is fairly well accepted that the idea originated in England, but the terminology of "open" began in this country. Like many other education theories, open education fell victim to the practice of taking a very complicated idea and reducing it to one very visible component and still expecting it to bring about the desired results. Unstructured classrooms, free exchange of children's ideas, and classrooms with no walls were tiny pieces of the idea of open education, but do not even begin to approach the complex intricacies of the philosophy. Postman and Weingartner (1973) make the following assertion:

> Americans have been especially interested in the experiments in Leicestershire, England, where teachers have developed a type of open classroom in which children move with relative freedom from one activity to another, in which there is little distinction between work and play, in which there is much opportunity for children to learn from each other, and in which there is a minimum of didactic teaching. Reports from England suggest that children are learning to read, calculate, and perform a wide range of other skills in such an environment. (181–82)

It is well known by those who study in the arts and social sciences that the values and mores of a society are reflected in the art, literature, and general culture of the society. Likewise, the manner in which a society chooses to educate its youth speaks volumes about what the society collectively believes and considers to be important. As such, it is easy to see the concept of education as democratic fitting nicely with most American ideals—inclusive rather than exclusive, cosmopolitan rather than provincial, comprehensive rather than narrow, fostering cohesion rather than division. Just as the initial emergence of progressive ideals came about when the country was rebuilding after some serious growing pains, it should come as no surprise that a serious movement toward progressive ideals began to surface in the mid 1960s when our country was in the midst of a massive Civil Rights movement that was long overdue. Bradley (1999) states, "As a movement, open education in the United States was clearly rooted in the political and social tumult of the times. It quickly became a cause for its adherents—many of them young teachers who had questioned authority in objecting to the Vietnam War, and who shared a reluctance to impose their wishes on students" (32).

Society was coming to realize that some things had to change, and that the schools had to become more inclusive and grow with the rest of society. Smith (1997) states,

To me it is no coincidence that open education should have become a significant movement in American education in the mid-'60's. The American
public had reached a higher level of consciousness about our social system
as it affects individuals, as it reflects social justice, and as it exercises social
control through its educational practices. I believe that open education is
part and parcel of the social spirit and impulse for liberation. . . . The major
thrusts of those persons reaching for social justice are toward (1) participation, (2) pluralism, and (3) liberation. (373)

The open education movement did not deliver as promised for several
reasons. School leaders and social thinkers of the time went to great extremes to rethink the meaning of school and to change the physical surroundings that had always been associated with schools. Unfortunately,
what did not change was the inherent ways in which schools function, the
ideas about what children are supposed to learn or how they should learn
it, and parents' perspectives on what school is supposed to do (Barth
1972). Most importantly, the problems, backgrounds, and experiences of
the children who attended schools did not and obviously could not
change. The problems and inadequacies that most children bring to school
did not change or go away simply because it was decided to massively re-
design the concept of instructional delivery. Simply creating school build-
ings, physical structures, and curriculum designs that embraced the ideas
of open education and expecting the rest of the world to change to meet it
is the same flawed logic as painting a wall that is supported by rickety or
inadequate framing. The new wall color cannot fix the problem behind the
wall or cause the wall to better serve its purpose.

There are other facets of the open education question to consider when
attempting to determine its demise; Postman and Weingartner (1973) clar-
ify this misconception as follows:

American adaptations of the British Infant Schools have been many and
various. For example, the "open corridor," introduced here by Lillian We-
ber, is an attempt to break away from the constricting presence of four walls
and a closed door by making the corridors and indeed all the space in a
school part of the learning environment. Unfortunately, in many places
classes are called open simply because the doors are kept that way, even
though instruction of the usual kind takes place. Of course, this is a perver-
sion of a good idea. Simply, a closed classroom becomes an open one when

its purpose is so satisfy the intellectual curiosity of children, instead of the requirements of a syllabus. If a teacher is not trying to do that, you will have a closed classroom, even if instruction takes place on 42nd Street and Times Square. (182)

Finally, Smith (1997) says the following in response to the question of "Did it work?":

> There was the natural tendency to say, simply, "Come and see! Isn't it wonderful?" If children are absorbed and happy, if busy activities seem to be going on, if wall displays show good quality work in art, graphs, charts, building plans, drawings, poems, written accounts of group projects, and so on, isn't that enough? Especially if the teacher can show you records for each child and how his or her individual work has developed over time? Not really, for those considering a change to open classrooms or for whom this was an entirely new approach. Nor was it enough for those concerned about what would happen to children when they graduated from an open classroom into the next, probably more formal stage of schooling. In short, did open education really "work"—and what did that mean? Or was it all really just mere playing around for the children before they got down to business? It was argued that well-to-do suburban children perhaps could afford such education, whether private or public, since they had plenty of background resources and opportunities for success later. But inner-city, "culturally disadvantaged" children could not: They needed "structure." (393)

INDIVIDUALIZED INSTRUCTION

There is a particularly popular idea that is coupled with particular verbiage and seems to fit nicely into the mind-set of democratic education geared to create productive citizens. Unfortunately, this idea—known generically as "individualized instruction"—like so many other generally good ideas that are assumed to correlate perfectly into the ideas of John Dewey, has been taken to such extremes as to lose any connection to reality. It is generally thought by most scholars of Dewey that the idea of "individual instruction" had far less to do with programs or curriculum intended for one person than a much bigger picture of a very humane mode of schooling that would support the individual. It can hardly be argued that the idea of providing a level of education that would support the individual thereby causing the individual to ultimately contribute their best to society is more what Dewey had in mind. It is further argued by many scholars of Dewey (Finn 1981) that Dewey made serious distinctions between education that could be considered "individualistic" (that which is imposed by external standards that compared one person against another) and education that was considered "for the individual" (that which capitalized upon the strengths, interests, and potential contributions of the individual). Finn (1981) states:

> Many "progressive" educational reformers at the turn of the century emphasized one or the other points of view. It seemed as if the choice were either more "education of individuals" within the tradition of individualism, or less "individualistic" education, an alternative to traditional liberalism. Those who responded to Dewey's call for more attention to individuals proposed schemes to "free" the child. Characterized as "I teach children, not math," this point of view, often combined with expressions of concern for the individual psyche, was accused by some of spoiling the child and softening the pedagogy. (253)

It is clear from his writings that Dewey indicated the idea of focusing the delivery of instruction toward the individual to be a philosophic phenomenon upon which to base practice and not a directive that would prove unworkable from a standpoint of either practicality or common sense. During the late 1960s and early 1970s, the idea of individualized instruction put into practice was often a literal attempt to design, develop, and implement a different program of instruction for every single child. Such efforts are remembered as the untold hours spent attempting to create such plans of instruction and all that is involved in what we have known for some time to be components of quality instruction. Generally, these types of efforts resulted in being discarded as simply unworkable. Others are remembered by prepackaged classroom materials that included "canned" instructional activities, supposedly sequenced and designed so that the student could unilaterally make the decision to complete the work, repeat the work, or go on—hardly what can be considered "interactive" as we know today. Likewise, the technology of the day consisted of audiocassettes—or perhaps filmstrips—that children could listen to in order to receive the help they needed to get past each step of the program. I recall such a math program being tried in my junior high school. The well-meaning teacher was excited when the principal released the funds (the amount of which was quite extravagant at the time) to purchase the program. The materials included the rather limited technological support of the day: eight audiocassettes, a player, and six large headphones (hardly the sleek, lightweight ones of today). The dry copier was not a technology readily available to teachers at the time nor had desktop computers been invented. Consequently, students worked from a "kit" where canned exercises were printed on cards. The teacher spent much of her time trying to keep the cards in order and answer questions as best she could. As only one tutorial audiocassette could be played at one time, many students would wait three to four class periods before their turn came to get the assistance they needed. My parents were among many who expressed their concern over some gross assumptions about individual progress when it was not clear that any progress was being made. Consequently, the program was short-lived. In retrospect, it cannot really be said that this experiment in individualized instruction did any particular degree of damage. From that class of children eventually emerged many responsible, well-prepared adults including teachers, attorneys, computer professionals, a physician, and the author of this book.

Most of us would not think John Dewey intended for this type of waste to occur in an effort to make education more democratic or to meet the needs of the individual. Clearly, such educational leadership behaviors were a gross misapplication of Dewey's ideas and the concept of education for the individual obviously gone amuck. Finn (1981) states,

Few, if any, "progressive education" reformers came close to Dewey's understanding and synthesis of the nature of man in social relations. Only the Lab School under Dewey's direction at the University of Chicago combined all three aspects of his thought: Reformism, romanticism, and scientism. Most other progressive reforms emphasized one or the other and were rightfully criticized as a result. The "socializers" (reformers) were criticized for neglecting the individual. Some claimed Dewey's ideal man was not more than a socially "good mixer." Others went farther and claimed the socializers were guided by a desire to promote better social control of the many by the few. Critics of the individualizers (romantics) complained of too much psychologizing and apologizing and too little learning and lack of concern for social problems. The influence of both was held responsible for what was said to be a general lowering of educational standards in the United States. (258)

THE POLITICS OF KNOWLEDGE

It is safe to assert that school reforms in general, and progressive education in particular, have not delivered as promised because the public has generally been skeptical and not supportive of such reform efforts over the years. We know that often what the public seems to demand is not quite what most people actually want (Stone 2000a). I am reminded of the old adage, "Be careful what you pray for—you may get it."

It is often assumed that the right to a free public education has been around as long as our country has been around. This is not so. The free public education that our society tends to take for granted only came about after years of work, struggle, and compromise. Apple (1990) states,

> No matter what some of our more well known social control theorists would argue, state funded schooling was not a "gift" given easily by dominant groups in society to control the minds of the people. Instead, such schooling was a *result* [italics in original] of concrete struggles among different groups with different social and cultural visions, and of course different resources and power. The form schooling took, the curriculum that was instituted, the way teaching went on, how and by whom it was controlled, all of this was the contradictory outcome of compromises or accords in which government had to respond to those "above and below" in the social structure. (377)

Although not a popular topic to confront, the schools, the working of the schools, and the services provided by the schools are all political questions. When it is quoted that education in this country is a "national concern, a state responsibility, but a local function" (Webb and Norton 1999), it stands to reason that school questions will invariably become political ones. The schools must serve the people who attend them. Therefore, it would make sense that most of what happens in schools is determined locally. State and federal governmental agencies only step in and get involved when their involvement becomes necessary, or when decisions must be made that cannot be made locally. It is the nature of political processes that decisions are made based on what is in the "general" best interest—meaning *most* people. The general best interest does not mean that everyone will get his or her way. As a professor of government once stated, it means that everyone gets a piece of the political pie, but some people will get a bigger piece than others.

Over many years we have seen the government step in when necessary but such involvement seems to have happened more in the past 50 years than probably the past 150. As states and federal agencies are continuing to step in during this era of standards and accountability, the questions to be posed are moving from "what is in the general best interest" to "what knowledge is the most valuable and who determines the value?" Marzano, Kendall, and Gaddy (1999) state,

> The promulgation of standards by groups of subject-area specialists who influence what is taught in virtually every classroom raises an interesting new question for American education: How long would it take for a student to acquire the knowledge that is defined as essential? . . . The answer, according to new research by the Mid-continent Regional Educational Laboratory, is that a high school diploma would require as much classroom time as has historically resulted in a master's or professional degree. Even the brightest students would need nine additional years of schooling to master the nearly 4,000 benchmarks experts have set in 14 subject areas. Subject-matter specialists and policy makers who have sought to clarify what students should learn have not considered the curriculum as a whole. The net result is a curriculum that is overwhelming to teachers and students. (68)

TOWARD INCLUSIVE SCHOOLS

When the schools expanded to include everyone, we also by default included all of the problems, inadequacies, and differences among people that come with such an effort. We are an industrialized nation that tries to educate every single child regardless of background, ability, or handicapping condition. Such an effort is most noble but not without some certain inherent drawbacks—particularly, that noble efforts often correlate quite nicely with naïveté. The naïve aspect of such a noble effort is the assumption that since we attempt to educate every child, the only determination of success is if we do actually succeed in educating every single child. No other professionals are held to such an unrealistic or naïve standard.

In the noble effort to make our schools more inclusive, the simple idea of reality seems to become overshadowed by the desirability of the ideology. Puolimatka (1996) states,

Alasdair MacIntyre [1984, 10] regards pluralistic society as too fragmented by conceptual diversity to sustain rational discourse. He claims that the public discourse of liberal democratic societies has degenerated into "an inharmonious mélange of ill-assorted fragments" which are incommensurable with each other so that mutual understanding has become an illusion. There is no neutral court of appeal to decide between rival moral claims since no particular conceptualization is used by all participants in the discussion. How then could there be critical evaluation and rational discussion? (7)

Perhaps educational leaders need to rethink the narrow and naïve idea of "inclusion." There is sometimes a fine line between forcing one's participation and allowing it.

READINESS FOR CHANGE

It is no secret that, concerning our schools, society was and has been ready for change for many years. Unfortunately, the schools have been unready and unable to facilitate change for several reasons. First, when we look back to the early 1900s, teachers had little or no formal training and equally little formal education. Society was tolerant of this at the time not because it was desired or because it truly met the needs of the youth of society, but because it was "good enough." Although there are many ill-informed (or possibly just mean-spirited) people who would disagree, today's teacher education is certainly better than it has ever been. Unfortunately, although teacher training has evolved with society, it has not kept up with society. As such, what we do to prepare teachers is still not enough. It is simply not possible to reform the schools and bring about the desired changes in society while the schools are struggling to put enough live, human adults in classrooms to see that children are not educating themselves. As the problems of society have expanded, so have the problems that come into the schools.

There is another unfortunate correlation to the question of readiness for change. Despite the efforts of all the learned societies and the abundance of standards from every conceivable direction, there are great discrepancies in how colleges of education interpret how to promote Dewey's ideas and bring about a mode of education that is democratic, practical, and available to the masses. Such reforms take time and are quite manpower intensive. Our schools are drowning in bureaucratic responsibilities and under intense political pressure to present immediate change—preferably, change that is nicely correlated with the next political cycle.

EDUCATING THE YOUTH IN A DEMOCRACY

When we read of John Dewey, the words *education* and *democratic* are almost inseparable, but this leads to another question that must be addressed. There are certain problems that will always be present when any services are provided for children and youth, but the problems of providing education to the youth of a democratic society are unique. Obviously those problems will be the same quite-universal problems found in the exercise of democratic society. Patrick (1998) has discussed this at length. This portion of the discussion focuses on his ideas.

According to Patrick (1998), there are three very general problems that exist both in the general exercise of democratic society as well as in the education for participation in a democratic society. These problems are:

1. Limits for majority rule
2. Limits for personal freedom and governmental power
3. Limits for positive rights (2)

In the exercise of democratic society, it is generally accepted that when it comes to decisions that influence everyone, the desires of the majority prevail—hence the idea of "majority rule." In most instances, even if the majority is only 51 percent, it is the desires of those 51 percent that influence what the remaining 49 percent must tolerate or at least live with. Obviously, someone is going to get a smaller piece of the political pie, and many will by necessity have to live with various choices they did not make. This practice prevails in the schools to a large extent, but not always as we see in the exercise of democratic society. The public schools are designed to be inclusive of exceptionalities to a much greater extent than society at large can ever be.

In addressing the question of personal freedom and governmental power, there must exist a positive and healthy balance between these two phenomena in order for democracy to work. But while society at large makes a most concerted effort to find and maintain that balance, that same balance really cannot exist in the schools for one reason: the clients served by the schools are children who have neither the legal autonomy nor social maturity to make decisions as it would be presumed of adults in a democratic society. In mainstream society, adults can make choices and be held accountable for those choices. This simply is not so with children.

In discussing the idea of limits for positive rights, Patrick (1998) determines positive rights as those things that the government can do for the individual. On balance, negative rights are those things that the government cannot force you to do or rights that cannot be taken away. Consequently, the schools cannot be exactly held to this standard because the service role of the schools is much different than the role that an ordered society plays in the life of the individual.

It is curious that most discussion of democracy in education never goes much further than a response of "Oh, . . . Dewey" or "Gee, that's nice." Somehow in the desire to make education more inclusive—hence, more democratic—we have lost sight of the fact that there will always be differences among people that cannot be realistically or theoretically allowed for. Lennes (1924) made the following statements concerning the concept of democracy and public education:

> One of the most far-reaching slogans of the past century has been: "Democracy must be educated." Now "democracy" includes all members of the *genus homo* who have reached a certain age, with the possible exception of some individuals so far below normal as to be classed as morons or lower. It is known of course, that, though all members of a democracy may be equal before the law, they are not equal either physically or intellectually. Indeed, the intellectual inequity of those who constitute democracy may not be appreciated as generally as it should be. . . . Hence it seems *a priori* probable that there is greater variation in mental aptitudes than there is in the general bodily powers which our ancestors have possessed during long geological ages. We must bear in mind that this variation extends downward from the average man as well as upward. But our school curricula have been devised with "democracy" in mind. We have provided stones to be placed in the educational wall which are not too heavy for the general fun of students and generally not too heavy for the weaker. It is not at all unlikely that our "curricula of easy tasks" owe their origin partly to a desire to provide an education which shall be "within the reach of all." And it may be that the

doctrine of "non-transfer of abilities which are developed by education" has been made use of to justify conditions which by itself it could not have brought about. When practical decision is rendered for reasons which would not be attractive if boldly stated, it is not uncommon to seek theoretical justification elsewhere. (33–34; italics in original)

MISAPPLICATIONS OF EDUCATIONAL RESEARCH

In any of the social/behavioral sciences, it is desired that professional decisions and behaviors are based upon the existing knowledge base. It is well known that the professions that provide the best services are those with the strongest knowledge base (Smith 1985). Ideas are tested systematically and the results are used not to drive the practice but to make decisions relative to furthering the practice. Most professions build upon what has been previously known by testing new ideas, tossing out what is not workable, and ultimately building a solid professional knowledge base. Unfortunately, this is not so in the business of public education, particularly in view of the prominent existence of progressive ideas (Grossen 1996a; Hirsch 1996, 2000, 2002). Due to the inherent inexactness of teaching and learning and particularly the frequent nebulous boundaries to progressive thinking (and teaching and learning in general), any kind of formal research that claims to empirically test the practices of democratic ideals will likely be suspect.

It is a great concern to scholars that far too many educational leaders claim support of various progressive ideas, usually attributable to Dewey in one form or another, and claim that support to be "based in research" or "research-based" (the very current educational nomenclature). Either claim is particularly problematic for educational scholars and practitioners for several reasons. First, there are varying definitions of the term *research* that mean slightly different things—none of which is inherently wrong. Definitions can vary from "systematic investigation" to "compiling existing literature" to "the gathering and reporting of opinions." Each can be considered correct in its own way and each genre is useful for making particular educational and policy decisions. Research in any field—even the pure and exact sciences—will always vary greatly in both style and quality. As such, a claim of "researched" does not necessarily mean studied in a scholarly context or is even indicative of any degree of quality. The further the definition moves from the idea of "systematically investigated," the less solid the basis for making decisions.

Second, the use of the term *research* or *researched* seems to lend a degree of scholarly or scientific credibility to the idea, regardless of whether such credibility might actually exist. Popular ideas are often coupled with the word *research* and come to be accepted as truth by novice and professional alike. It is quite alarming how frequently one hears persons in positions of leadership quote a passage, cite an idea, or comment on a topic only to find that person is misinformed, half-informed, or just blatantly in error. This leads to the next problem.

Third, popular ideas tend to hang around for a long time. Consequently, many popular but inherently wrong ideas are complacently accepted as truth when they are, in fact, merely common opinion. As such, educators are directed (essentially forced) to use methods that have no professional standing (Goodman 1998; Weinig 2000). Most such ideas are rooted in good intentions and a well-meaning desire to provide the best for our children. But in this context, one is reminded of the old colloquialism, "The road to hell is paved with good intentions."

When I teach graduate courses in research at the university, one of the first and most basic tenets I present is the fact that research does not "prove." When one hears a speaker or consultant use the words *research* and *prove* in the same sentence, it is safe to assume that either research findings are being misapplied or the person does not understand what research means and does not mean. Research findings represent the aggregate, not the anecdote. As such, one set of findings that contradicts all previous findings is not wrong, nor are all previous findings called into question. (E. D. Hirsch would discuss this question as "consensus research.") Although we use research findings to build our knowledge base, research findings indicate tendencies, never absolutes. Findings and data lend support or credence to an idea, but can never be considered "proof" one way or another.

There are numerous contemporary scholars who speak out in concern for the plight of legitimate scholarly research in education, or more specifically, the lack of use of legitimate research (Miller 1997). It has long been my argument, and one of the tenets of this book, that we often see complex ideas falter because of research findings either misapplied or pushed outside the

bounds of common reason. Slavin (1987) cautions educators to be skeptical
of popular ideas that appear quickly and equally quickly are being implemented, in various forms, on a large scale. Grossen (1996b) admonishes educational leaders to be aware of and reject ideas that go from "idea to professional knowledge base" with nothing in between. Stone and Clements
(1998) caution educators to be aware of fads masquerading as reform and
to be highly critical and skeptical of frequently made claims that seem logical but on closer examination are easily seen to be flawed.

The most prominent professional squabble that will likely never be re-
solved is the question of qualitative versus quantitative research. In brief,
qualitative data tends to be more descriptive in nature while quantitative
tends to be more numerical or measurable in nature. Consequently, when
we have extremes in definitions, we tend to have extremes in beliefs. One
segment of the professional population believes that only quantitative
findings yield useful information because they are "exact." The other segment believes that quantitative findings are too rigid to be useful in the social sciences, which by their inherent nature are quite inexact. Occasion-
ally, those of us whose belief falls somewhere between the two are looked
upon as "indecisive" or "unscholarly." Who wins this battle? Concerning
the qualitative/quantitative squabble, Hirsch (2002) says,

> Education-school proponents of "qualitative" research criticize quantitative
> research by taking note of the variability of classroom contexts, and claim-
> ing that all education, like all politics, is local. (They use the term "situated
> learning.") They pride themselves on following "ethnographic" methods,
> and taking into account the uniqueness of the classroom context. They
> rightly object that quantitative research tries to apply oranges to apples. But
> if their descriptions do not disclose something general that I could confi-
> dently apply to my own classroom, their studies are not very useful. And if
> their inferences did have general application, then the value of an "ethno-
> graphic" rather than a straightforward general description would lie in the
> literary vividness of a concrete example. But literary value is rarely claimed
> or observed in these productions. (7)

It surprises many students new to research to learn that not all research
is good (Kinnaman 1993). Much of what makes it to print each year can be
found to be flawed, skewed, biased, insignificant, "fluff," or even outright
wrong. The point to be stressed here is that while we know what makes

good and bad research, relatively little is discussed in professional writing as to how frequently policy decisions are made based on flawed or questionable findings, or even information that is simply incorrect. Consequently, we see programs implemented and directives issued that do not consider the population being served or the inherent problems the populations bring to their school experiences. Even worse, we find directives issued because such is the ideological choice of those issuing the directives. The most unfortunate aspect of this dilemma is how often such misapplication bears the name or is somehow attributed to Dewey. Equally unfortunate is how frequently such misapplications are called "progressive" when in fact they are nothing of the sort. Smith (1985) makes the following observation about educational research and the subsequent policy implications:

> Periodically, U.S. society experiences a peculiar phenomenon—an overwhelming drive, almost a frenzy, for school reform. A few prominent citizens become anxious about the quality of schooling and express themselves in loud complaints about teachers, teaching, soft pedagogy, softer curricula, or whatever. These movements quickly lose their momentum after a few changes are introduced—courses modified, methods refurbished, course requirements altered, laws enacted. Each begins with a bang and ends about where it began. (689)

There is a good body of information to support the idea that teachers are more effective when they have been taught the tenets and ideals of traditional research (White and Gary 2000). Grossen (1996a), a serious proponent of quality research for schools, makes the following point:

> Unfortunately, we are still a long way from achieving such a system. Many of the educational practices that are widely touted by academic theorists and teacher-training programs across the country don't even have Level II support, never mind Level III. When these practices fail, however, who gets blamed? Not the promoters and publishers who sold unworkable materials; not the well-paid consultants who provided the staff development and implementation advice; not the university professors who developed the theory. Teachers are blamed. If it doesn't work, "The teachers didn't do it right." To request Level II and III research support is just to ask that instructional practices not be foisted on schools before it had been shown if and how they work. Today, this assurance cannot be taken for granted. (23)

As educated professionals, the responsibility is ours alone to know the body of literature relative to our profession. Most practitioners in any field do not necessarily need to hold particularly refined statistical or research skills but instead need to hold a broad understanding of research processes so that they are prepared to make good decisions based on what research actually says. Whether we are discussing educators, medical professionals, mental health workers, or even those called to the ministry, it is generally known that conducting research is seldom part of the practitioners' work, mostly for reasons of time. This is not a weak link in the practitioner/researcher realm, for many times it is far more important that the practitioners be prepared to interpret current research findings rather than create new ones. The cycles of bad decisions based on bad information will not stop until our practitioner workforce makes it happen.

Chapter Five

Making Progressive Education Work: Perspectives, Conclusions, and Recommendations

> It would be easy to write off this debate as an all-too-predictable exer-
> cise in rhetorical wheel spinning, but to do so would be sad and fool-
> ish, for these two traditions represent the best we know about teaching
> and learning.
>
> —D. B. Ackerman, 2003

We have seen from the reviews of perspectives and the comparisons presented in this book that the question of progressive education is not one in
which there is an easy and concise answer. We have seen repeatedly that many
ideas that came forth with the most honest of intentions have gone bad—not
because the ideas were bad, but because the ideas became misplaced in an attempt by well-meaning people to serve the segment of the population whom
they perceived as the most in need. It should be clear from the presentation in
this book that progressive education has not failed the people but that, in fact,
people have failed progressive education. Cassidy (1980) states,

> For many years the popular perception of Dewey tended to be a caricature,
> in which his concern for democracy and his belief that it should permeate
> the educational process was seen as an attack on all adult authority in the
> schools, and as an apology for mindless permissiveness. More recently this
> picture has been substantially revised by historians of education, and Dewey
> and other progressive educators are not accused of sacrificing democracy to
> social control and manipulation. (5)

But how is it that such a well-intended, seemingly attainable idea has gone
amuck? What must the leaders of today do in order to realistically see the

philosophies of progressive education perform as they were intended? My argument is that in order for progressive education to do as it was intended, there must be a balance between extremes. Similarly, Egan (1999) states,

> One or another form of progressivism has been promoted and tried in the schools of North America since the beginning of mass schooling in the latter part of the nineteenth century. Usually, progressivist practices have been promoted on the grounds that if only teachers will attend to the new knowledge gained by research about learning or development and follow what the research implies for teaching or curricula, an educational revolution will take place. Each new generation of progressivist educators has, first, to explain what was wrong with his or her predecessors' attempts to implement the ideas—because the promised revolution consistently fails to occur—and then explain why her or his new approach will do the job. (11)

I think a particularly effective view of the progressive/traditional question as it relates to the democratic presentation for the common people comes from my childhood and our home. Lawrence Welk was a musician, performer, artist, and conductor whose contribution to the American musical culture was unparalleled. His musical style was a presentation that put the culture of the common people to a higher level and as such would appeal to the more artistically sophisticated sector of society. I do not know if Lawrence Welk had the background and requisite skills, nor would he have been comfortable, even particularly competent, with performing the more serious levels of classical music (orchestra, operatic, etc.). He did, however, have a remarkable skill at raising the level of sophistication in his presentation of musical theater and dance through his skill as an arranger and conductor, and in orchestration. This was evidenced not only by the huge popular following of Lawrence Welk and his work but also by the people whom he chose to perform in his orchestra and chorus—all of whom were consummate professional performers in their own right. When we watch the reruns of the shows that were recorded in the 1960s and 1970s, the performers chosen by Welk were clearly trained in the classical techniques, and clearly were educated in music at least at the university or conservatory level.

Even if the style of Lawrence Welk and his performers does not particularly meet the taste of the individual, there can be no question that his performers were clearly as trained in traditional classical performance practices as any others. The level of competence of Welk's performers is evidenced by what was the only available technology of the day. At that time, there was no such thing as digital technology that allowed sound engineers to modify sound. When Lawrence Welk's musicians performed, the blend and balance the public heard was true blend and balance that can only be brought about by skill and repetitious practice (the kind of practice that progressive education is reputed to hold in disdain), not the electronic modification of sound as today's sound technicians can do. How then does the analogy of Lawrence Welk's success as a musician serve to exemplify the traditional/progressive question? Let us make two points:

1. This genre of American culture was of a level that it could only be achieved (performed or understood) by those who at least had an appreciation, if not cognitive understanding, of performance practiced at the classical level.
2. This genre of American culture allowed a sector of the American public to enjoy this level of musical sophistication when some years earlier, this type of cultural enjoyment would only have been available to the elite of society.

The bottom line here is that if progressive education is ever to be expected to work, the same two elements must be in place as those that caused Lawrence Welk and his efforts to succeed. First, everything about progressive education—the beauty, the enjoyment, the inclusive nature—must have the traditional (collections of skills brought about by a collective body of information and supported by repetitious drill and practice) as the backing. Second, the progressive must be of the same quality as the traditional (held to conventional standards), but focused to a different sector (inclusive) without sacrificing quality. This all translates to one simple idea—progressive education is a broad collection of generic ideas, not one extreme pitted against another. Dewey (1938) cautioned educators in this regard:

> Mankind likes to think in terms of extreme opposites. It is given to formulating its beliefs in terms of *Either-Ors* [emphasis in original] between which it recognizes no intermediate possibilities. When forced to recognize that the extremes cannot be acted upon, it is still inclined to hold that they are all right in theory but that when it comes to practical matters circumstances compel

us to compromise. Educational philosophy is no exception. The history of
educational theory is marked by position between the idea that education is
development from within and that it is formation from without; that it is
based upon natural endowments and that education is a process of overcom-
ing natural inclination and substituting in its place habits acquired under external pressure. (26)

PERPETUAL QUESTIONS

In looking at the idea of perpetual questions, Prawat (1997) says, "Dewey
realized that swings in the education pendulum, signifying child- or
learner-centered instruction in one decade and a return to fact- and skill-
based learning in another are symptomatic of a deeper philosophical problem: the separation of mind and body and mind and world" (2).

I have well supported the argument that there is unquestionably a war
between ideologies. In our business, it seems as though scholars prefer to
argue over ideas rather than processes or procedures that are known to
work or not work (Carnine 2000). Just as in unresolved marital disputes,
this type of unproductive arguing causes the pendulum to swing, with the
direction of the swing being determined by those who scream the loudest.
As such, I would then pose two questions relative to the idea of making
progressive education work:

1. Does there truly need to be a winner in this ideological war? This battle has raged on for over a century and is similar to the fights that go
   on in bad marriages or relationships.
2. Does embracing a different idea necessitate totally rejecting any and all
   other? (It would appear that doing so perpetuates the extremism that
   we know is not a good idea and that Dewey admonished.)

I believe the answer to both of these questions is a resounding "no." For
some reason, however, there seems to exist a mind-set that only in the extreme is an idea useful. Pogrow (1997) states,

So we are left with ideological progressives talking about professional development as an individualistic process with teachers and students sponta-
neously making the right decisions, while the competition, ideological con-

servatives, talk only about drill, vouchers, and school prayer. There is no basis for a dialogue. While the two ideologies compete for their moment in the
limelight, education practice vacillates between periods where drill rules
and where total fuzziness rules. The extremes on both ends of the spectrum
such as the available funding and use of government policy and foundation
support to control the public agenda and debate. As a result, education stag-
nates. . . . Progressive education has been hurt by the fact that those controlling the agenda place a premium on ideology and care more about
process than outcome. (4)

Some writers claim a balance is necessary. Others claim the two extremes can never meet. Still others claim that one extreme or another is
closely related to quality business practices (Sevick 1999). A thorough
overview of the literature reveals that the "never mix" idea seems to dominate (Carr 1998). This is problematic for one reason. According to Apple
(1990), effective decisions about curriculum and instruction must be neutral. But there is an inherent attribute of neutral that can never be perfect
because there can never be a universal definition of "common good"
(Strike 1988). No organization that provides a service can ever be totally
neutral because being so would mean that the organization either had no
purpose or that the purpose was quite unclear. Strike (1988) states,

Any society that wishes to be a free society but that also wishes to have a
population that supports its central moral commitments has a dilemma to re-
solve. On the one hand, such a society must respect the diversity of its citizens and their diverse visions of a good life. At the same time, it must promote a core of common democratic principles. . . . Such a society will have
to address two questions. First, it will need a coherent view about what it
may rightfully promote and what it must leave to the discretion of its members. Second, it will need to establish institutions that competently promote
those principles that may rightfully be promoted but that avoid encroaching
on the individual's sphere of discretion. (256)

STRIVING FOR PERFECTION

Several years ago I purchased and renovated a historic home (1883)—a
project I would never have imagined I would pursue. Although many details of the outcome were less than perfect in many ways, it was still quite

beautiful and my work contributed significantly to the value and historical integrity of the home as well as the community. As I was working on the home and diligently striving to stay within time, budgetary, and building-permit restraints, I had many well-meaning friends (and strangers) tell me "how things should be done." It seems as though everyone has his own idea about how to renovate an old home, even if he had never done so or would not have to live in the results.

Likewise, almost everyone has her own idea as to what a quality education should be about. Naturally, everyone wants a system of education that will best serve his needs and will perpetuate his way of life (Brantlinger and Majd-Jabbari 1998). In our free-market economy, middle-class Americans have become a "spoiled" group of people who are quite accustomed to having their way in most matters that affect their daily lives and seem to live under a mind-set of entitlement, especially when it comes to matters of schooling (Dodd 1998; Kohn 1998). While we know that a basic tenet of psychology is the idea that caring for one's personal well-being does not indicate a disregard for others, we are generally unwilling to make small personal sacrifices that will benefit everyone in the long term. We hear many people argue for more and more services of the schools that involve greater and greater expense, yet we find few people willing to support the necessary human effort or tax increases that will finance such reforms. Unfortunately, everyone seems to both want and expect a system of education that will be perfect for everyone every time even though common sense dictates that such will never happen. We see large numbers of well-meaning citizens calling for reform not on the basis of overall betterment of the system, but on self-serving ideologies (Kohn 1998). Beyer (1988) states,

> The further stratification of school people must be reversed not only within the teaching force but in our relations with students as well. Current efforts to identify and design special environments for the "talented and gifted," the "emotionally disturbed," the "learning disabled," and so on, are usually well intentioned by practitioners. Yet they frequently have the effect of segregating students on the basis of pseudo-scientific procedures and language that makes broad-based participation and self-governing activities problematic. In furthering inequalities of opportunity and status, they bolster the tendencies of liberalism and thin democracy. This is not to deny that individuals and groups are often aided by programs that provide special facilities or per-

sonnel. Yet it is imperative that such programs not isolate or stigmatize teachers and students in ways that jeopardize their membership in the school community and their opportunities for self-governance. (268)

Our schools are inundated with the perfectionist ideals linked with the concept of cultural pluralism. In an effort to serve most, there seems to have emerged a mind-set that if enough clearly established rules are put in place, then the needs, wants, and desires of everyone can be met every single time with no one left out. This is particularly problematic when we consider the overpowering mind-set that seems to be imposed on the public schools that would never be imposed on any other providers of social services—the idea that if one person, or a reasonable percentage of persons, are not served well, the entire system is at fault. Such mind-sets do not exist in the practices of medicine, law, psychology, or physical therapy—all of which are as imperfect as teaching and learning. Only educators tolerate the imposition of such double standards.

When academic and casual conversation turns toward the schools and the workings therein, we frequently hear "Well, when I went to school . . ." It is interesting that this perspective comes forth from people of all ages, backgrounds, and levels of education. As a university professor, I often hear undergraduate students lament how deplorable situations have become in recent times. I am privately amused to hear an undergraduate student of nineteen years speak of the "old ways" when in all likelihood they were a student in those public schools not more than three years earlier. It's difficult to imagine that circumstances in the public schools could have evolved or changed for the worse in that short a period of time. Perhaps the "when I was in school" syndrome is really a matter of well-intended individuals recalling what they currently consider to be the desired.

SHALLOW FAMILIARITY

There is an old saying that "a little education can be a very dangerous thing." This old adage is intended not to criticize but to caution well-meaning individuals that a shallow understanding of a deep question can lead to more problems than solutions. It is an unfortunate fact of life that this is seen probably more frequently in the practice of public education than any other profession. In previous writings I have discussed numerous extreme examples of educational leaders in prominent places who made seriously erroneous decisions based on blatant misinformation. As a university professor of educational administration and leadership, I feel the pressure every day to see and know that prospective educational leaders and school principals do actually demonstrate a scholar's perspective of the issues and ideas. The average educational consumer does not recognize that the practice of education, while dealing with the intellect, will never be a matter that can be approached logically, worked out systematically, and come out with no loose ends or unexplained phenomena. Teaching and learning are simply too imperfect to expect such. As educational leaders, we must recognize and absolutely reject the attitude of simplicity we so often see graphically displayed in the mass media today—usually surrounded by meaningless political verbiage that hurls blame at the practitioner force. Hampel (1999) states,

> It is not an easy task to read, discuss, and use the ideas in the major books on education. Unlike a university seminar, it is hard to establish one interpretation as better than another. Who in the faculty is privileged to do so? There are few teachers who know the concepts so deeply that they can call attention to unthoughtfulness, misinterpretations, and other lapses in the conversations. Those who do may hold back for fear of sounding preachy and bossy. . . . In place of debate, teachers often try something new, tell colleagues it worked well, and one then pushes to see if in fact the innovators performed as well as advertised. Colleagues congratulate each other for their willingness to experiment. (45)

I will make another musical analogy to demonstrate the idea of shallow familiarity. Some years ago when the philosophies of Zoltan Kodaly were coming to the forefront of the world of music education, I witnessed a number of individuals who claimed to be "Kodaly educators" because they taught the traditional system of solfege and used hand signals as a support for sight singing. This idea and conception of music education in practice was a very superficial application of the activities that are a manifestation of the ideas behind the philosophy—but with no grounding in the philosophy. It is interesting that the persons who truly learned the methods and philosophies of Kodaly are still practicing music educators today. Those who learned the surface sorts of activities have long since moved on to other shallow misunderstandings. Such has clearly been the case with progressive education. It is disheartening to see school administrators and other educational leaders make flagrantly erroneous statements under the guise of progressive ideals that common sense would dictate come nowhere near what John Dewey would have intended.

But such problematic phenomena do not exist solely around the question of progressive education, Dewey, and democratic education. It is a concern among many, myself included, at how little usable or generally valuable professional information gets passed from the ranks of academe to the trenches where children are actually being taught.

ANOTHER VISIT TO ANIMAL FARM

Old sayings that hang around for years do so because of the seeming universal applicability of the pieces of wisdom or the philosophical threads to which they are attached. One such saying is that the "half-educated can be far more dangerous than the uneducated." Practitioners must know the professional body of literature before they can ever be prepared to make effective decisions. If practitioners or leaders are ever to be in a situation whereby they can bring about positive change, the leadership force must be educated in the issues beyond a superficial level. It is unfortunate that most of us have seen the "surface" level of understanding far more often than we have seen the "in-depth" level of understanding. In the same manner in which the narcissistic pigs on Manor Farm managed to control the entire animal population by keeping them half-informed of the "big picture," so it is frequently seen in the schools. Ideas or practices that are only marginally related to the ideas of John Dewey are presented as the unerring gospel and presented in such a manner as to assume that anyone who thinks differently is somehow "wrong." In the same manner in which the Orwellian pigs assured the animal population that all decisions were made in the best interest of all concerned, so it is in the schools. Those who think for themselves will often hear what the animals heard: "Snowball was responsible for this . . ." or "Do you want Farmer Jones to come back?" By keeping the workforce in a state of quasi-hysteria, they are more easily controlled under the mind-set of "Don't think for yourself, let us think for you." Withholding information is an easy way to control people.

The surface level of understanding tends to manifest itself in short-term solutions that often are not solutions at all but instead are the academic counterpart of a bandage on a compound fracture. Dayton (1995) makes the following comparison:

> An epidemic of short-term orientation is at the heart of many of American society's most serious problems. Environmental destruction, the creation and disbursement of carcinogens, chemical, and nuclear wastes, the spread of AIDS, deficit spending, neglect of children's basic needs, and many other problems that threaten to diminish or destroy the hopes of future generations are dependent on the decisions of current policy makers and the citizens they represent. But the danger these predicaments present to a society whose vision is limited by short-term orientation is that these issues will only become critical during the tenure of future policy makers and citizens. Short-term oriented policy makers continue to ignore the lessons of the past, and deny their responsibility in creating the future. Decisions are made as if in a temporal vacuum, neither guided by the past nor concerned with the future. As Barber (1992) recognized: "Our incapacity to think imaginatively or constructively or responsibly about the future—whether in economics, environment, social security, family planning, energy management, nuclear proliferation, crime, or, above all, education—has its origin at least in part in our historical obliviousness, our incomplete sense of ourselves in time (p. 35). (140)

In my own experience I have seen some glaring, half-educated misapplications of Dewian ideals, particularly at the middle-school level. As educational leaders, we must always call for an explanation when we see gross misapplications, such as:

- Critical content deleted from courses because "the children don't enjoy it." Dewey repeatedly warned of the need for content first, everything else second.
- Forcing one's teaching into thematic areas. Several years ago I saw a probably well-intended central office administrator issue a directive that all classrooms were to design all teaching around four thematic areas, one each grading period. It seemed ludicrous at the time that several hundred teachers at various grade levels could realistically manage and design the instruction for an entire grading period around such themes

as "earth" or "friends." Despite the directive, the idea did not work particularly well, mostly because it was a bad idea and a misinterpretation of philosophies.

SOME POINTS TO CONSIDER

In the century-long argument for and against the ideas and tenets of progressive education, the question of "the science of learning" has always been present. It is argued obtusely that if scientific principles are applied to the work and workings of the schools, then we will see positive results, in the same manner that scientific models of industrial efficiency are applied to business and industry. Although it is erroneously assumed to be a turf problem, those of us who work in this business do not agree for many reasons. Let us examine the following model.

There are essentially three levels of science. They are:

- *Theoretical/Exact Sciences*—which include various fields of mathematics and engineering. This level of science is best described as being based on a collective body of information that is generally accepted by and agreed upon by those in the profession. The body of information does not change. The tenets of the body of information are quite concrete, quite observable, and quite measurable.
- *Pure/Applied Sciences*—which include such fields as biology, geology, chemistry, and so forth. This level of science is likewise easily described as being based on a collective body of information that is generally accepted by and agreed upon by those in the profession. Generally, the body of information does not change. The tenets of the body of information are quite concrete, quite observable, and (generally) quite measurable.
- *Behavioral/Social Sciences*—which include such fields as psychology, sociology, economics, anthropology, and education. This level of science is based on a body of information that is generally accepted by those in the profession. But, unlike the other levels of science, the body of information is constantly changing and evolving, primarily because studies in these areas are relatively new by comparison. Unlike the other levels of science, the behavioral/social sciences are not particularly measurable.

Study in the theoretical/exact or pure/applied sciences can be organized in a systematic manner. Because of their exact nature, it is logical and realistic to assume that if we perform a certain procedure we are assured of a certain outcome. We have enough years of collective data to know that certain mathematical and engineering tenets can be accepted as truth, even if the tenet itself isn't quite absolute. We know that relationships exist between certain foods and behaviors and certain problems in biology. We know that the absence of certain behaviors and substances relate to biological phenomena as well. But certain tenets of the more exact science can never apply to teaching and learning. We may be able to state with reasonable certainty that a particular amount of force is necessary to get a stone of a certain weight up a hill of a certain slope. We can know that the same amount of force will be required for the same size stone on the same slope every single time we attempt to push the stone. Regardless of how logical it may seem, however, we cannot and will never know that a person of a certain age, size, and physical stature will in fact be able to push that stone at any given time until we see them do so. There are simply too many factors to be considered that somehow influence whether the person can or will push the stone.

It is clear from this model of the sciences that to attempt to approach and study the behavioral/social sciences in the same manner as one would approach and study the other sciences simply will not work. The non-measurable qualities of the behavioral/social sciences makes such efforts suspect from the start. But in the same manner of the Orwellian pigs, the idea continues to float around that such tenets are exact. This is where the average educational consumer misses the point.

The three levels of science illustrated in this model do not exist or "operate" in isolation or even separately from one another. Just as the collective knowledge base in the pure/exact sciences supports the practice of medicine, so it is with teaching and learning. A mastery of the massive body of biological, chemical, and technical knowledge does not in and of itself constitute the practice of medicine. The practice of medicine is providing services and making decisions that are in the best interest of the individual using the supporting body of knowledge as the basis for such decisions. Clearly, one cannot function without the other.

A physician cannot logically assume that a certain process, procedure, technique, or medication will work every time for every person. This is true for the educators as well. In the field of mathematics, we know that the same operation will always produce the same result. However, it is naïve and dangerous to assume that one operation will produce the same outcome in the practice of medicine or the practice of teaching. Yet for some reason, that exact, precise, one-size-fits-all mind-set continues to prevail.

DEMOCRATIC IDEAS AND CURRENT ACCOUNTABILITY PRACTICES

Our nation is in the midst of what will undoubtedly be discussed in thirty years the way the pseudo/quack reforms of the 1960s are discussed today. According to Eberstadt (1999), some dozen years [1981–1993] of Republican administration and the supposed adherence to conservative ideals has brought about an era of "'standards,' 'testing,' 'achievement,' and other terms regarded by progressives as ideological fighting words" have become the common nomenclature in our business (1). The notion of "accountability" is the current and ever-so-prominent buzzword but like many other reforms in our business, a consensus (or even commonsense agreement) has yet to surface. The idea behind the accountability movement is twofold:

1. By forcing the schools to publish performance data to be read by the general public, no one is able to hide in the inherent bureaucratic entanglement and the public is fairly informed as to how well public dollars are being used.
2. With nowhere to hide, schools and school leaders will be forced to produce, improve, or shut down.

It would appear that this was a fair thing to do and on the surface might seem relatively easy to accomplish. Unfortunately, a mixture of myth and misunderstanding comes forth when we realize that the means of accounting to the public is virtually the exclusive use of standardized test scores. The public has been grossly misled by the patently false idea that we can somehow legislate success. The threat of shutting down schools over test-score performance is ludicrous and will never happen because of the social ramifications if not the practical. One can only imagine the social outcry should the children from a "failing" school be shipped to the high-performing school several miles away. Doing so does not fix the problem, it only redistributes it. It is doubtful that educational leaders and parents of the "high-performing children" will embrace the idea of "lower-performing children" being immersed into their ranks, thereby pulling down their averages and status.

It is fair to assert that in the accountability wars, we have not found educators—progressive or otherwise—who are opposed to the idea of being held fairly accountable to the public for the work they do and the results they produce. Likewise, it is fair to assert that educators of repute would welcome the opportunity to put their work before the public if such could be done in a fair and ethical manner and in such a medium as to present a real, not politically accentuated, picture of what we do. But doing so would necessitate the media presenting some very unpopular political opinions, particularly as it relates to the sociological factors that no one wants to admit actually exist—the extreme dichotomy of the haves versus the have-nots. The real attack on educational accountability programs that is justifiably coming from the ranks of professional educators is focused on the use of standardized test data as the sole determinant of quality.

Let us return to the bottom-line definition of democracy: meaningful participation by everyone. The current accountability movement in the state where I reside—while being hailed by some and chastised by others—is nowhere near this definition. Forcing educators to publish information and data to a public that generally does not know what that information means is the modern Orwellian equivalent of the alleged rule-breakers in puritanical New England being placed in the stocks in the square. The scoffing public is able, even encouraged, to mock and jeer with no understanding of why the person is there and an inadequate amount of information to make an informed choice or judgment. This does the same damage as the unkind, ill-informed neighbor who perpetuates neighborhood gossip.

It is argued by many—and I do not necessarily discount those perspectives—that the accountability wars are being fueled by an erroneous mind-set that exists among society at large. There is an almost self-perpetuating belief that anyone with a desire to teach can do so and do so effectively. With the nationwide shortage of teachers at critical levels, it should be clear that few people really choose teaching because they are unable to do anything else. It is fair to say that most people choose teaching out of a genuine desire to make a difference and improve the quality of life for others. But another mind-set prevails that is more prevalent in teaching than in other service professions. It is commonly believed that only in teaching children are there problems, discrepancies, and inefficiencies. Nothing could be further from the truth. Whether we are teaching small children, adolescents, college undergraduates, graduate students, law students, or medical students, there will always be a common body of attributes that we know make for good teaching. Regardless of the level of teaching, there will always be "problem children"—those whose learning styles and other personal attributes add difficulty to the work of the teacher. When I became a university professor after many years in the public schools, I was quite naïve in thinking that I would never have to require graduate students to resubmit inferior work. The very same decisions must be made when teaching graduate students or medical students as teaching elementary school children. Stitham (1991) makes the following comparison in medical school teaching:

> Part of the arrogance of medicine is the idea that receiving an MD degree means acquiring an instant ability to teach. Teaching requires instruction in educational techniques. Teaching takes personnel, time, and money. But when the faculty's primary obsession is whether that NIH grant is coming through to pay their salaries or whether their latest article has been accepted so they can get tenure, teaching will never get the time it deserves. (906)

AN ALIGNMENT ORGY: FORCE-FIT OF GOOD IDEAS

In this book I have discussed many and varying aspects of good ideas gone bad because of a well-intended but misguided intent to force an idea to work where common sense and logic would say otherwise. As educational practitioners and leaders, we must become literate of the professional knowledge base so that we will know good information from bad and essentially good decisions from bad. In this mind-set, Mason (1996) states,

> The success of potentially good ideas in education depends on how classroom teachers enact them. Jacobs suggests that interdisciplinary teaching

is now so widely accepted that it represents *good mainstream education* [emphasis in original] rather than a peripheral force (Kiernan, 1993). If this is so, why are there not more good examples of integrated instruction in schools? Jacobs may be correct that there is little dispute that an integrated curriculum can provide advantages such as those cited above, but serious obstacles exist to the successful widespread implementation of this idea. (266)

I have quoted the above to bring forth the point that the educational world has gone crazy with some near-quack rendition of the idea of alignment—the force-fit of every thought, idea, practice, or phenomenon to "touch" in order to create a seamless system. This alignment orgy is the outgrowth of the misapplied idea of relevance. Although most academic subject matter is somehow linked, it is naïve and mis-educative (to coin a Dewey term) to assume that no academic discipline ever stands alone. In our current practices, however, we are seeing some bizarre connections in the same manner that using the existing wardrobe and attempting to never duplicate an outfit will eventually create some strange, probably distasteful, combinations. As a public school teacher in very recent years, I recall the pressure from well-meaning but misinformed educational leaders to link daily instruction across disciplines. Lesson plan forms were created that forced the teachers to "correlate" what was being taught to something else—possibly everything else.

The great misfortune here—and the crux of the fate of progressive education—is that every time this idea is forced, we find the same disappointing results. Invariably we find some strange combinations that defy accepted practice, logic, common sense, or even good taste.

References

Ackerman, D. B. 2003. Taproots for a new century: Tapping the best of traditional and progressive education. *Phi Delta Kappan* 84 (5): 344–49.

Adler, M. 1939. The crisis in contemporary education. *Social Frontier* 5 (42): 140–45.

Adwere-Boamah, J., D. H. Delay, and O. C. Jones. 1982. Fundamental points of view of teachers on education: An investigation of Kerlinger and Kaya attitudinal scale. *Educational Research Quarterly* 7 (2): 17–20.

Anderson, W. L. 2000. The legacy of progressivism. *Thought You Should Know.* www.tysknews.com/Depts/gov_philosophy/legacy_of_progressivism.htm (accessed May 14, 2003).

——. 2002. Lott: The progressivist legacy continues. *Lew Rockwell.com.* www.lewrockwell.com/anderson/anderson60.html (accessed May 14, 2003).

Anfara, V. A., and L. Waks. 2000. Resolving the tension between academic rigor and developmental appropriateness. *Middle School Journal* 32(2): 46–51.

Anyon, J. 1980. Social class and the hidden curriculum of work. *Journal of Education* 162 (1): 67–92.

——. 1981. Social class and school knowledge. *Curriculum Inquiry* 11 (1): 3–42.

Apple, M. W. 1990. The politics of official knowledge in the United States. *Journal of Curriculum Studies* 22 (4): 377–83.

Archer, J. 2002. National board is pressed to prove certified teachers make difference. *Education Week* 21 (20): 1, 11.

Attwood, P., and J. Seale-Collazo. 2002. The toolbox and the mirror: Reflection and practice in "progressive" teacher education. *Radical Teacher* (Fall): 14–22.

Ayers, W. 1990. Rethinking the profession of teaching: A progressive option. *Action in Teacher Education* 12 (1): 1–5.

Bagley, W. C. 1921. Dangers and difficulties of the project method and how to overcome them: Projects and purposes in teaching and learning. *Teachers College Record* 22 (4): 288–97.

Baines, L. 1997. Future schlock: Using fabricated data and politically correct platitudes in the name of educational reform. *Phi Delta Kappan* 78 (7): 492.

Baker, B. 1998. Child-centered teaching, redemption, and educational identities: A history of the present. *Educational Theory* 48 (2): 155–74.

———. 1999. The dangerous and the good? Developmentalism, progress, and public schooling. *American Educational Research Journal* 36 (4): 797–834.

Barber, B. R. 1992. *An aristocracy of everyone: The politics of education and the future of America*. New York: Ballantine.

Barth, R. 1972. *Open education and the American school*. New York: Agathon Press.

Beane, J. A. 1998. Reclaiming a democratic purpose for education. *Educational Leadership* (October): 8–11.

Beinecke, J. A. 1998. A progressive at the pinnacle: William Heard Kilpatrick's final years at Teacher's College Columbia University. *Educational Theory* 39 (2): 139–49.

Bernardo, A. S. 1996. American education at the crossroads. *New York Eagle Forum.com*. www.newyorkeagleforum.org/esteem/esteem_articles/crossroads (accessed February 5, 2004).

———. 1997. Educational reform: Dumbing down or emasculation? *New York Eagle Forum.com*. www.eagleforum.org/educate/1998/feb98/focus.html (accessed February 5, 2004).

Bernstein, R. J. 1966. *John Dewey*. Atascadero, Calif.: Ridgeview Publishing.

Beyer, L. E. 1988. Can schools further democratic practices? *Theory into Practice* 27 (4): 263–69.

Black, D. L. 2000. Progressive education means business. *Education Week* 20 (13): 36, 39.

Blair, J. 2001. New accreditor gaining toehold in teacher education. *Education Week* 20 (37): 1, 12, 13.

Bly, R. 1990. *Iron John: A book about men*. New York: Addison-Wesley.

Bond, L. 1998a. Validity and equity in the assessment of accomplished teaching: Studies of adverse impact and the National Board for Professional Teaching Standards. Paper presented at the annual conference of the American Educational Research Association, San Diego, Calif.

———. 1998b. Disparate impact and teacher certification. *Journal of Personnel Evaluation in Education* 12 (2): 211–20.

Bond, L., R. Jaeger, T. Smith, and J. Hattie. 2000. *The certification system of the National Board for Professional Teaching Standards: A construct and consequential validity study*. Greensboro: Center for Educational Research and Evaluation, University of North Carolina.

Bradley, A. 1998. Alternative accrediting organization taking form with federal assistance. *Education Week* 17 (3): 22.

————. 1999. Open to innovation. *Education Week* 18 (32): 32–33.

Bradley, J. 1998. Muddle in the middle. *Education Week* 17 (31): 38–42.

Brantlinger, E., and M. Majd-Jabbari. 1998. The conflicted pedagogical and curricular perspectives of middle-class mothers. *Journal of Curriculum Studies* 30 (4): 431–60.

Bredekamp, S. 1987. *Developmentally appropriate practice in early childhood programs serving children from birth through age 8*. Washington, D.C.: National Association for the Education of Young Children.

Bredekamp, S., and S. Copple. 1997. *Developmentally appropriate practice in early childhood programs serving children from birth through age 8*. Washington, D.C.: National Association for the Education of Young Children.

Bredekamp, S., and T. J. Rosegrant. 1992. Reaching potentials through appropriate curriculum: conceptual frameworks for applying the guidelines. In *Reaching potentials: Appropriate curriculum and assessment for young children*, edited by S. Bredekamp and T. J. Rosegrant, 28–42. Washington, D.C.: National Association for the Education of Young Children.

Burnett, J. R. 1979. What ever happened to John Dewey? *Teacher's College Record* 8 (2): 192–210.

————. 1988. Dewey's educational thought and his mature philosophy. *Educational Theory* 38 (2): 203–11.

Burroughs, R. 2001. Composing standards and composing teachers: The problem of national board certification. *Journal of Teacher Education* 52 (3): 223–32.

Burroughs, R., T. A. Schwartz, and M. Hendricks-Lee. 2000. Communities of practice and discourse communities: Negotiating boundaries of NBPTS certification. *Teacher's College Record* 102 (2): 311–71.

Bybee, R. W. 1998. The Sputnik era: Why is this educational reform different from all other reforms? *National Academy of Sciences*. www.nas/edu/sputnik/bybeel.htm (accessed February 5, 2004).

Callahan, C. 1981. Education for democracy: Dewey's illiberal philosophy of education. *Educational Theory* 31 (2): 167–74.

Callahan, R. E. 1971. George S. Counts: Education statesman. In *Leaders in American Education*, edited by R. J. Havighurst. The 77th yearbook of the National Society for the Study of Education. Chicago, Ill.: University of Chicago Press.

Carnine, D. 2000. Why education experts resist effective practices (and what it would take to make education more like medicine). *Thomas B. Fordham Foundation*. www.fordhamfoundation.org/library/carnine.html (accessed May 13, 2002).

Carr, D. 1998. Traditionalism and progressivism: A perennial problematic of educational theory and policy. *Westminster Studies in Education* 21:47–55.

Cassidy, K. M. 1980. John Dewey and the problem of authority. ERIC no. ED187627.

Chall, J. S. 2000. *The academic achievement challenge: What really works in the classroom*. New York: Guilford.

Chall, J. S., V. A. Jacobs, and L. E. Baldwin. 1990. *The reading crisis: Why poor children fall behind*. Cambridge, Mass.: Harvard University Press.

Childs, J. L. 1956. *American pragmatism and education*. New York: Henry Holt.

Chipman, D. D., and C. B. McDonald. 1980. The historical contributions of William Heard Kilpatrick. *Journal of Thought* 15 (1): 71–83.

Chung, S., and D. J. Walsh. 2000. Unpacking child-centeredness: A history of meanings. *Journal of Curriculum Studies* 32 (2): 215–34.

Cohen, D. K. 1998. Dewey's problem. *Elementary School Journal* 98 (5): 427–46.

Coleman, J. S. 1991. What constitutes educational opportunity? *Oxford Review of Education* 17 (2): 155–59.

Connell, L. 1963. Child-centered or subject-centered? *Bulletin of the Institute of Education, University of Leads*, no. 42.

Coughlan, N. 1975. *Young John Dewey: An essay in American intellectual history*. Chicago: University of Chicago Press.

Cuban, L. 1983. How did teachers teach, 1890–1908? *Theory into Practice* 22 (3): 159–65.

———. 1990. Reforming again, again, and again. *Educational Researcher* 19 (1): 3–14.

Cunningham, G. K. 2001. The culture of progressive education and the culture of the traditionalists. *Education News*. www.EducationNews.org (accessed May 11, 2001).

Darling-Hammond, L., and J. Snyder. 1992. Reframing accountability: Creating learner-centered schools. In *The changing contexts of teaching*, edited by A. Lieberman, 11–36. Ninety-first Yearbook of the National Society for the Study of Education, Part 1. Chicago: University of Chicago Press.

Dayton, J. 1995. Democracy, public schools, and the politics of education. *Review Journal of Philosophy and Social Service* 20 (1): 135–156.

DeBoer, G. E. 1998. What we have learned and where we are headed: Lessons from the Sputnik era. *National Academy of Sciences*. www.nas.edu/sputnik/deboer.html (accessed February 5, 2004).

Delpit, L. 1996. *Other people's children: Cultural conflict in the classroom*. New York: New Press.

Dewey, J. 1900. *The school and society*. Chicago, Ill.: University of Chicago Press.

———. 1902. *The child and the curriculum*. Chicago, Ill.: University of Chicago Press.

———. 1910. *How we think*. Boston: Heath.

———. 1916. *Democracy and education*. New York: Macmillan.

———. 1938. *Experience and education*. New York: Macmillan.

Dodd, A. W. 1998. What can educators learn from parents who oppose curricular and classroom practices? *Journal of Curriculum Studies* 30 (4): 461–77.

Doll, W. E. 1983. A re-visioning of progressive education. *Theory into Practice* 23 (3): 167–73.

Donovan, C. F. 1951. Dilution in American education. *America* 86 (November 3): 121.

Eakin, S. 2000. Giants of American education: John Dewey, the education philosopher. *Technos: Quarterly for Education and Technology* 9 (4). www.technos.net (accessed August 7, 2003).

Eberstadt, M. 1999. The schools they deserve: Howard Gardner and the remaking of elite education. *Policy Review*. www.policyreview.org/oct99.eberstadt .html (accessed September 17, 2002).

Egan, K. 1999. The myth of progressivism: Robustly wrong ideas we have inherited from Herbert Spencer, John Dewey and John Piaget. *Faculty of Education, Simon Fraser University*. www.educ.sfu.ca/kegan/FlawIntro.html (accessed May 10, 2002).

Englund, T. 2000. Rethinking democracy and education: towards an education of deliberative citizens. *Journal of Curriculum Studies* 32 (2): 305–13.

Entwistle, H. 1970. *Child-centered education*. London: Methuen.

Feinberg, W., and J. Odeshoo. 2000. Educational theories in the fifties: The beginning of a conversation. *College of Education, University of Illinois at Urbana-Champaign*. www.ed.uiuc.edu/EPS/Educational-Theory/Contents/ 2000_3.asp (accessed February 5, 2004).

Finn, M. E. 1981. Education innovation and Dewey's moral principles in education. *Educational Studies* 12 (5): 251–63.

Gallant, T. F. 1973. Dewey's child-centered education in contemporary academe. *Educational Forum* 37 (4): 411–19.

Garrett, A. W. 2000. *Beyond "An experiment with a project curriculum": The other works of Ellsworth Collings*. ERIC no. ED 448125.

Gay, K. 1986. *Crisis in education: Will the United States be ready for the year 2000?* New York: Franklyn Watts.

Generals, D. 2000. Booker T. Washington and progressive education: An experimentalist approach to curriculum development and reform. *Journal of Negro Education* 69 (3): 215–34.

Goodman, K. S. 1998. The phonics scam: The pedagogy of the absurd. *Talking Points* 10 (1): 8–10.

Goodman, P. 1969. Visions of the school in society. In *Radical school reform*, edited by R. Gross and B. Gross. New York: Simon and Schuster.

Grinberg, J. G. A. 2002. I never had been exposed to teaching like that: Progressive teacher education at Bank Street during the 1930s. *Teacher's College Record* 104 (7): 1422–60.

Gross, R. E. 1989. Reasons for the limited acceptance of the problems approach. *Social Studies* 80 (5): 185–86.

Grossen, B. 1995. Overview: The story behind Project Follow Through. *Effective School Practices* 15 (1). www.uoregon.edu/~adiep/ft/grossen.htm (accessed February 5, 2004).

———. 1996a. Making research serve the profession. *American Educator* 24 (2): 4–9.

———. 1996b. What does it mean to be a research-based profession? *University of Oregon.* http://darkwing.uoregon.edu/bgrossen/resprf.htm (accessed November 12, 2000).

———. 1998. Child-directed teaching methods: A discriminatory practice of western education. *University of Oregon.* http://darkwing.uoregon.edu/bgrossen.cdp.htm (accessed December 10, 2000).

Gutmann, A., and D. Thompson. 1996. *Democracy and disagreement.* Cambridge, Mass.: Harvard University Press.

Halasz, P. 1990. Growing up progressive. *Virginia Quarterly Review* 66 (1): 104–27.

Hampel, R. L. 1999. The power and peril of idea driven reform. *Education Week* 18 (32): 44–47.

Hillerich, R. L. 1990. Whole language: Looking for balance among dichotomies. ERIC no. ED 315746.

Hirsch, E. D. 1996. *The Schools We Need and Why We Don't Have Them.* New York: Doubleday.

———. 1997. Why Traditional Education Is More Progressive. *American Enterprise.* www.taemag.com/issues/articleid.16209/article_detail.asp (accessed February 5, 2004).

———. 2000. Conservative education policies would benefit public schools. In *Education: Opposing viewpoints*, edited by M. Williams. San Diego, Calif.: Greenhaven Press.

———. 2001. *Romancing the child.* www.coreknowledge.org (accessed May 13, 2002).

———. 2002. Classroom research and cargo cults. *Policy Review*, no. 15. www.policyreview.org/OCT02/hirsch_print.html (accessed May 13, 2002).

Hlebowitsh, P. S., and W. G. Wraga. 1995. Social class analysis in the early progressive tradition. *Curriculum Inquiry* 25 (1): 7–21.

Holland, R. 2002a. Findings prompt scrutiny of national certification board. *Heartland Institute.* www.heartland.org/education/aug02/findings.htm (accessed March 21, 2003).

———. 2002b. National certification: Advancing quality or perpetuating mediocrity? *Lexington Institute.* http://lexingtoninstitute.org (accessed March 21, 2003).

Holt, M. 1994. Dewey and the "cult of efficiency": Competing ideologies of the 1920s. *Journal of Advanced Composition* 14 (1): 73–92.

Hunter, E. 1985. Under constant attack: Reflections of a teacher educator. *Phi Delta Kappan* 67 (3): 222–24.

Iheoma, E. O. 1997. Rousseau's views of teaching. *Journal of Educational Thought* 31 (1): 69–81.

Irvine, J., and J. W. Fraser. 1998. Warm demanders. *Education Week* (May 13), 35.

Jesness, J. 2000. The legacy of progressive education. *SpeakOut.com.* www.speakout.com/activism/opinions/2971-1.html (accessed February 5, 2004).

Johnson, D. D., and B. Johnson. 2002a. *High stakes: Children, testing, and failure in American public schools.* Lanham, Md.: Rowman and Littlefield.

———. 2002b. The unfairness of uniformity. *Reading today: International Reading Association.* www.reading.org/publications/try/0208_unfair.html (accessed February 5, 2004).

Johnson, J. A., V. L. Dupuis, D. Musial, G. E. Hall, and D. M. Gollnick. 1999. *Introduction to the foundations of American education.* Boston: Allyn and Bacon.

Kahne, J. 1995. Revisiting the Eight-Year Study and rethinking the focus of educational policy analysis. *Educational Policy* 9 (1): 4–23.

Kaplan, A. 1997. Public life: A contribution to democratic education. *Journal of Curriculum Studies* 29 (4): 431–53.

Katz, M. B. 1971. *Class, bureaucracy, and schools: the illusion of educational change in America.* ERIC no. ED 061388.

Kesson, K. 1999. Experience and education. *Education Week* 11 (7): 57, 73.

Kiernan, L. J. 1993. *Integrating the curriculum* [video]. Alexandria, Va.: Association for Supervision and Curriculum Development.

Kinnaman, D. E. 1993. Research in education: approach with caution. *Technology and Learning* 14 (2): 78.

Kliebard, H. M. 1985. Three currents of American curriculum thought. *Current Content on Curriculum: 1985 ASCD Yearbook.* Arlington, Va.: ACSD, 31–44.

———. 1986. *The struggle for the American curriculum 1893–1958.* Boston: Routledge.

Knoll, M. 1996. Faking a dissertation: Ellsworth Collings, William H. Kilpatrick, and the "project curriculum." *Journal of Curriculum Studies* 28 (2): 193–222.

Kohn, A. 1998. Only for my kid: How privileged parents undermine school reform. *Phi Delta Kappan* 79 (8): 568–77.

———. 1999. *The schools our children deserve: Moving beyond traditional classrooms and "tougher standards."* Boston: Houghton-Mifflin.

Lennes, N. J. 1924. *The teaching of arithmetic*. New York: Macmillan.

Levin, H. M. 1981. *Education and organizational democracy*. ERIC no. ED 207218.

Levin, R. A. 1991. The debate over schooling: Influences of Dewey and Thorndike. *Childhood Education* 68 (2): 71–75.

Loveless, T. 1997. The second great math rebellion. *Education Week*. www .edweek.org/ew/vol-17/07love.h17 (accessed May 13, 2002).

MacIntyre, A. 1984. *After virtue*. Notre Dame, Ind.: University of Notre Dame Press.

Marzano, R. J., J. S. Kendall, and B. B. Gaddy. 1999. Deciding on "essential knowledge." *Education Week* 18 (32): 68.

Mason, T. C. 1996. Integrated curricula: Potential and problems. *Journal of Teacher Education* 46 (4): 263–70.

Matczynski, T. J., J. F. Rogus, T. J. Lasley, and E. A. Joseph. 2000. Culturally relevant instruction: Using traditional and progressive strategies in urban schools. *Education Forum*, 64 (4): 350–57.

McAninch, A. C. 2000. *Continuity and purpose in the design of meaningful project work*. ERIC no. ED 439856.

Meier, D. 2000. Progressive education policies would benefit public schools. In *Education: Opposing viewpoints*, edited by M. Williams. San Diego, Calif.: Greenhaven Press.

Miller, D. W. 1997. The black hole of educational research. Why do academic studies play such a minimal role in efforts to improve schools? *Chronicle of Higher Education*. www.chronicle.com/weekly/v45/i48/48a00101.htm (accessed July 7, 2002).

Mirochnik, E. 2003. The centerless curriculum. *Teacher Education Quarterly* 29 (4): 73–78.

Moore, D. M. 1999. The National Board for Professional Teaching Standards (NBPTS) assessment: Learning styles and other factors that lead to success. PhD diss., University of Cincinnati, Ohio.

Nadler, R. 1998. Low class: How progressive education hurts the poor and minorities. *National Review* (December 21), 31.

Nash, G. B. 1995. The history standards controversy and social history. *Journal of Social History* 29 Suppl.:39–50.

National Council for Accreditation of Teacher Education. 1999. *Program standards for elementary teacher preparation (review and comment edition)*. Washington, D.C.: NCATE.

Nehrig, J. 2001. Certifiably strange. *Teacher Magazine* 13 (1): 49–51.

Norris, N. D. 2002. *Perspectives on the mistreatment of American educators: Throwing water on a drowning man*. Lanham, Md.: ScarecrowEducation.

———. 2003. Connecting child-centered teaching and the middle school concept. *Louisiana Middle School Journal* 14 (1). www.lmsaonline.org/jourcont.htm (accessed February 5, 2004).

Ogden, W. R. 1992. The progressive education association: Gone but not forgotten. *College Student Journal* 26 (3): 281–84.

Olson, D. R., and J. Bruner. 1996. Folk psychology and folk pedagogy. In *The handbook of education and human development: New models of learning, teaching, and schooling*, edited by D. R. Olson and N. Torrence, 9–27. Cambridge, Mass.: Blackwell).

Olson, L. 1999a. Tugging at tradition. *Education Week* 18 (32): 25.

———. 1999b. Dewey: The progressive era's misunderstood giant. *Education Week* 18 (32): 29.

Pahl, R. H. 2001. The social studies of Harold Ordway Rugg. *Social Studies* 92 (2): 53.

Partington, G. 1987. The disorientation of Western education: When progress means regress. *Encounter* 68 (5): 5–15.

Patrick, J. J. 1998. *Three universal problems of democracy at the core of education for democratic citizenship*. ERIC No. ED425095.

Perlstein, D. 1996. Community and democracy in American schools: Arthurdale and the fate of progressive education. *Teachers College Record* 97 (4): 625–50.

Petrosky, A. R. 1994. Schizophrenia, the national board for professional teaching standards' policies, and me. *English Journal* 83 (7): 33–42.

Pipho, C. 2000. A new reform model for teachers and teaching. *Phi Delta Kappan* 81 (6): 421–22.

Plank, D. N., R. K. Scotch, and J. L. Gamble. 1996. Rethinking progressive school reform: Organizational dynamics and educational change. *American Journal of Education* 104 (2): 79–102.

Plowden. 1967. *Children and their primary schools: Report of the Central Advisory Council for Education*. London: HMSO.

Podgursky, M. 2001a. Should states subsidize national certification? *Education Week* 20 (30): 38, 40, 41.

———. 2001b. Defrocking the national board. *Education next*. www.education next.org/20012/79.html (accessed April 29, 2002).

Pogrow, S. 1997. The tyranny and folly of ideological progressivism. *Education Week*. www.edweek.org/ew/ew_printstory.cfm?slug=12pogrow.h17 (accessed May 13, 2002).

Pool, J. E., C. D. Ellett, S. Schiavone, and C. Carey-Lewis. 2001. How valid are the national board of professional teaching standards assessments for predicting the quality of actual classroom teaching and learning: Results of six mini case studies. *Journal of Personnel Evaluation in Education* 15 (1): 31–48.

Postman, N., and C. Weingartner. 1973. *The school book: For people who want to know what all the hollering is about.* New York: Delacorte Press.

Prawat, R. 1997. Fuzzy math, old math, and Dewey. *Education Week* (December 10). www.edweek.org/ew/ew_printstory.cfm?slug=16prawat.h17 (accessed May 13, 2002).

Puolimatka, T. 1996. Democracy, education and the critical citizen. *College of Education, University of Illinois at Urbana-Champaign.* www.ed.uiuc.edu/EPS/PES-yearbook/96_docs/puolimatka.html (accessed August 11, 2002).

Radcliff, B. 1992. Majority rule and impossibility theorems. *Social Science Quarterly* 73 (3): 511–22.

Radest, H. B. 1983. Progressive education revisited. *Education Week.* www.edweek.org/ew/ew_printstory.cfm?slug=03210001.h02 (accessed May 13, 2002).

Ravitch, D., and C. E. Finn Jr. 1987. *What do our 17-year-olds know?* New York: Macmillan.

Redefer, F. L. 1948. What has happened to progressive education? *Education Digest* 14 (1): 49–52.

Rotberg, I. C., M. Hatwood-Futrell, and J. Lieberman. 1998. National board certification: Increasing participation and assessing impacts. *Phi Delta Kappa International.* www.pdkintl.org/kappan/krot9802.htm (accessed February 5, 2004).

Rowland, V. R. 1951. My adventures as a teacher. *Sign* 31 (October): 34–37.

Rugg, H. O. 1939. Curriculum-design in the social sciences: What I believe. In *The future of the social studies*, edited by J. A. Michener, 140–58. Cambridge, Mass.: National Council for the Social Studies Curriculum Series.

Sachs, P. 1996. *Generation X goes to college: An eye-opening account of teaching in postmodern America.* Chicago: Open Court.

Sclan, E. M. 1990. *Curriculum-making of the child-centered progressive educators: Contraposed to Dewey's theory of experience.* Paper presented to the American of Educational Research Association, 1990. ERIC no. ED341139.

Schubert, W. 1986. *Curriculum: Perspective, paradigm, and possibility.* New York: Macmillan.

Schugurensky, D., and N. Aguirre. 2002a. 1919: The progressive education association is founded. In *History of education: Selected moments of the 20th century*, edited by D. Schugurensky. http://fcis.oise.utoronto.ca/~daniel_schugurensky/assignment1/1919pea.html (accessed November 1, 2002).

———. 2002b. 1930: The Eight-Year Study begins. In *History of education: Selected moments of the 20th century*, edited by D. Schugurensky. http://fcis.oise.utoronto.ca/~daniel_schugurensky/assignment1/1930eight.html (accessed September 13, 2003).

Sedlak, M. A., and S. Scholssman. 1985. The public school and social services: Reassessing the progressive legacy. *Educational Theory* 35 (4): 371–83.

Semel, S. F., and A. R. Sadovnik. 1999. *Schools of tomorrow, schools of today: What happened to progressive education?* New York: Peter Lang.

Sevick, C. V. 1999. Total quality education and progressive education: Are they related? *Catalyst for Change* 128 (2): 14–16.

Sewall, G. T. 2000. Lost in action: Are time-consuming, trivializing activities displacing the cultivation of active minds? *American Educator* 24 (2): 4–9.

Shanker, A. 1996. The importance of civic education. *Issues of Democracy* 1 (8). http://usinfo.state.gov/journals/itdhr/0796/ijde/shanker.htm (accessed May 10, 2002).

Shapiro, M. S. 1983. *The child's garden: The kindergarten movement from Froebel to Dewey.* University Park: Pennsylvania State University Press.

Shepard, L. A. 1995. Using assessment to improve learning. *Educational Leadership* 52 (5): 38–43.

Slavin, R. E. 1987. The pet and the pendulum: Faddism in education and how to stop it. *Phi Delta Kappan* 70 (10): 752–58.

Smith, B. O. 1985. Research bases for teacher education. *Phi Delta Kappan* 66 (10): 685–90.

Smith, L. H. 1997. "Open education" revisited: Promise and problems in American educational reform (1967–1976). *Teachers College Record* 99 (2): 371–415.

Stern, B. S., and K. L. Riley. 2001. Reflecting the common good: Harold Rugg and the social reconstructionists. *Social Studies* 92 (2): 56.

Stitham, S. 1991. Educational malpractice. *Journal of the American Medical Association* 266 (7): 905–6.

Stone, J. E. 1999. Will teacher training reform led by the schools of education improve student achievement? Not likely. Policy Brief, the Foundation Endowment. *Heartland Institute.* www.heartland.org/pdf/2180el.pdf (accessed July 13, 2002).

———. 2000a. Aligning teacher training with public policy. *State Education Standard* 1 (1): 35–38.

———. 2000b. The National Council for the Accreditation of Teacher Education: Whose standards? *Education Consumers Clearing House.* www.education-consumers.com/articles/whose_standards.shtm (accessed June 29, 2002).

———. 2001. Will teacher training reform led by the schools of education improve student achievement? *Association of American Educators.* www.aaeteachers.org/training.htm (accessed February 5, 2004).

———. 2002. The value-added achievement gains of NBPTS-certified teachers in Tennessee: A brief report. *Education Consumers Clearing House.* www.education-consumers.com/briefs/StoneNBPTS.shtm (accessed September 14, 2002).

Stone, J. E., and A. E. Clements. 1998. Research and innovation: Let the buyer beware. In *The superintendent of the future*, edited by R. R. Spillane and P. Regnier. Gaithersburg, Md.: Aspen Publishing.

Stout, M. 2000. *The feel-good curriculum: The dumbing down of America's kids in the name of self-esteem*. San Francisco: Perseus Books.

Strike, K. A. 1988. Democracy, civic education, and the problems of democracy. *Theory into Practice* 27 (4): 256–61.

Tanner, L. N. 1997. *Dewey's laboratory school: Lessons for today*. New York: Teacher's College Press.

Telhaug, A. O. 1990. *Den utdanningspolitiske retorikken* [The new rhetoric of education policy]. Oslo: Universitetsforlagert.

Townsend, B. 1988. What's at stake? Educational levels in the U.S. *American Demographics* 10 (8): 10.

Tyack, D. 1975. The high school as a social service agency: Historical perspectives on current issues. *Educational Evaluation and Policy Analysis* 1 (September–October): 45–57.

Vandervoort, F. S. 1983. What would John Dewey say about science teaching today? *American Biology Teacher* 45 (1): 38–41.

Vergari, S., and F. M. Hess. 2002. The accreditation game. *Education Next* 2 (3): 48–57.

Walker, J. C. 1981. Two competing theories of personal autonomy: A critique of the liberal rationalist attack on progressivism. *Educational Theory* 31 (3, 4): 285–306.

Walkerdine, V. 1984. Developmental psychology and child-centered pedagogy. In *Changing the subject*, edited by J. Henriques et al. London: Methuen.

Watkins, C. L. 1995. Follow through: Why didn't we? *Effective School Practices* 15 (1). Briefing. www.education-consumers.com/briefs/feb2001.shtm (accessed February 5, 2004).

Webb, L. D., and M. S. Norton. 1999. *Human resources administration: Personnel issues and needs in education*. Columbus, Ohio: Prentice-Hall.

Weiner, L. 2000. Democracy, pluralism, and schooling: A progressive agenda. *Educational Studies* 31 (3): 212–24.

Weinig, K. M. 2000. The 10 worst educational disasters of the 20th century: A traditionalist's list. *Education Week* 19 (40): 31.

Weissglass, J. 1999. Curriculum and society. *Education Week* 18 (32): 45, 47.

Westbrook, R. B. 1991. *John Dewey and American democracy*. Ithaca, N.Y.: Cornell University Press.

Westhoff, L. M. 1995. The popularization of knowledge: John Dewey on experts and American democracy. *History of Education Quarterly* 35 (1): 27–47.

White, E., and T. Gary. 2000. *Changing teaching practices by empowering teachers with research knowledge*. ERIC No. ED 448130.

Wichmann, T. F. 1980. Babies and bath water: Two experiential heresies. *Journal of Experiential Education* 3 (1): 6–12.

Wilson, J. 1991. Education and equality: Some conceptual questions. *Oxford Review of Education* 17 (2): 223–30.

Winter, E. 1997. Polishing the progressive approach. *Education Week* (April 16).

Wise, A. 1989. Calling for "national institutes of education." *Education Week* 9 (7): 36.

Withers, W. 1937. Is progressive education on the wane? *School and Society* 46 (September 25): 401–3.

Wood, E. 1990. Reforming teaching: Is it possible? *Education Canada* 30 (4): 28–35.

Wright, D. 1990. School leaders question costs, competition of nationally certified teachers. *School Administrator* 47 (2): 22–25.

Zilversmit, A. 1984. Progressivism in the Midwest. *History of American Education Quarterly* 24 (2): 257–60.

———. 1993. *Changing schools: Progressive education theory and practice, 1930–1960*. Chicago, Ill.: University of Chicago Press.

Index

About the Author

Norman Dale Norris has worked in public education for more than twenty years as a choral director at all levels, classroom teacher, teacher trainer, and university professor. As a passionate advocate for the performing arts, he prepared many award-winning choral ensembles over the years. Dr. Norris holds undergraduate and master's degrees in music education and piano, and a doctorate in school management and instructional leadership.

Dr. Norris is an assistant professor of education at Nicholls State University (Thibodeaux, Louisiana) where he teaches graduate courses in research, foundations, and school administration. Additionally, he continues to advocate for the arts by teaching undergraduate courses in music education.

Dr. Norris resides in New Orleans, Louisiana, is the father of a teenage daughter, and enjoys social and cultural events as well as historic home restoration. This is his second book.